Blessed Are We

EXPERIENCING JOY AS THE BEATITUDES OF JESUS TURN OUR PRIORITIES UPSIDE DOWN

LeRoy Lawson

STANDARD PUBLISHING

Cincinnati, Ohio

Library of Congress Cataloging-in-Publication Data

Lawson, E. LeRoy
    Blessed are we / LeRoy Lawson.
        p.   cm.
    Includes bibliographical references.
    ISBN 0-7847-0749-9
    1. Beatitudes—Criticism, interpretation, etc. I. Title

BT382.L34 1998
241-5'3—dc21   97-40009
                                                           CIP

Edited by Theresa C. Hayes.
Cover design by Barry Ridge Graphic Design

The Standard Publishing Company, Cincinnati, Ohio.
A division of Standex International Corporation.

05 04 03 02 01 00 99 98   5 4 3 2 1

Table of Contents

1

Before the Blessing
Comes the Prioritizing

But seek first his kingdom and his
righteousness, and all these things will be given to you
as well. Therefore do not worry about tomorrow, for tomorrow
will worry about itself. Each day has enough
trouble of its own.
Matthew 6:33, 34

If you're like me, your first few readings of the beatitudes left you pretty confused. What Jesus calls blessings
didn't sound like anything I wanted to receive:
    Blessed are the poor in spirit
    Blessed are those who mourn
    Blessed are the meek
    Blessed are those who are persecuted . . . .
What are we to make of a teacher who thinks it's a good

thing to be poor, somehow wonderful to be in mourning, praiseworthy to be without power, and that being persecuted is something to be desired?

What are we to do, we modern Americans caught in a culture that shrieks at us, "You can have it all" when our Lord quietly orders us to "seek first the kingdom of God"—where you probably will have very little that your countrymen think is so valuable? Who's right? Whom do we follow?

Perhaps our difficulty lies not so much in the beatitudes as in our priorities. Maybe our expectations are just not quite what they should be. If we don't value the things God values, we won't know a blessing from God when we see one. We'll be like Frank and Ernest in a recent cartoon, telling the parson, "I'm tired of blessings in disguise—if it's all the same to you, I want one I can recognize immediately!"[1]

But how will they recognize it? How can they possibly think of their poverty or persecution as a blessing unless they have somehow learned to think like Jesus, to make his priorities their priorities? There is no way around this truth: Before the blessing comes the prioritizing.

Establishing one's priorities is what the apostle Paul urges every believer to do: "Set your hearts on things above, where Christ is" (Colossians 3:1). *Above*—that's the problem. The Lord seems so far above us that it's hard to see or hear him over the din of ads and commercials and promises of every kind.

Still Jesus challenges, "What good is it for a man to gain the whole world, yet forfeit his soul?"(Mark 8:36). What are you really after, pilgrim? What kind of profit are you chasing? For Paul the choice is easy: "One thing I do. . ." (Philippians 3:13). For me it's more truthful to say, "These many things I'm trying, admittedly not too successfully, to do. . . ."

Jesus admits that prioritizing isn't easy. In fact, he deliberately makes it sound unattractive: "If anyone would come after me, he must deny himself and take up his cross and follow me" (Matthew 16:24). Self denial and crossbearing are not the most appealing options we can think of.

For that matter, Paul doesn't make it sound any too alluring, either: "Endure hardship with us like a good soldier of Christ Jesus" (2 Timothy 2:3). Is hardship soldiering what we signed on for when we became disciples of Christ?

We turn for relief from these disturbing orders to Jesus' comforting counsel in the Sermon on the Mount. Don't worry, he advises. Consider the lilies of the field, the sparrows of the air. God takes care of them. You don't need to fret. Your heavenly Father knows everything you need and he'll take care of you too.

You'd think that Matthew 6:25-34 would be called the Great Beatitude. For most of us, nothing sounds more blessed than to be free of worry. But before the blessing comes the prioritizing, remember? In the paragraph just ahead of these soothing words, Jesus lays the foundation for the blessed, worry-free state he recommends:

> For where your treasure is, there your heart will be also.
>
> The eye is the lamp of the body. If your eyes are good, your whole body will be full of light. But if your eyes are bad, your whole body will be full of darkness. If then the light within you is darkness, how great is that darkness!
>
> No one can serve two masters. Either he will hate the one and love the other, or he will be devoted to the one and despise the other. You cannot serve both God and Money.
>
> Matthew 6:21-24

We've come right back to putting first things first, again. If money is your concern, worry will be your life's companion. If God is, then his kingdom and his righteousness will be your first priority—and "all these things will be given to you as well."

Lifelong questions

We begin thinking about our priorities as children.
What do I want to be when I grow up? Or do? Or have?
These questions don't go away when we become adults. I
was still asking them in my forties. For that matter, now
that my contemporaries are racing into retirement, the
questions have come back again with a vengeance. What
do I want to do with my remaining years? Shall I preach,
shall I teach, shall I try for things beyond my reach?
There's a difference in my questioning now, though. Long
ago I opted for his kingdom and his righteousness, so the
main things have been decided.

And the result?

The testimony of most long-time Christians I know is
like mine. We could fill a catalogue with the blessed surprises we've enjoyed because many years ago we decided
to follow Jesus.

Our experience parallels Simon Peter's in Luke 5:1-11.

The teacher's general instructions

It was a pretty typical day for Jesus, standing along the
lakeside, a growing mass of people crowding him closer
and closer to the water's edge until he spotted relief. He
climbed aboard one of the boats and addressed the crowd
a short distance out from the shore. He already knew the
owner, more formally called Simon, but the same man we
know more familiarly by the nickname Jesus later gave
him, Peter.

We aren't told the subject of the Lord's discourse that
day. Peter himself probably soon forgot, the preaching
overshadowed by the unforgettable object lesson that followed.

As I was writing these paragraphs, there was a knock at
the front door. One of our church members dropped by for
a little counsel. His question was a big one: "How do we
know the will of God?" I steeled myself for the lengthy

dissertation I was about to deliver on the subject, when he narrowed the topic considerably. He didn't want general instructions; he had just come from dealing with a dishonest employee. The man had been stealing from him, then lying about his stealing. My friend had disciplined him while at the same time giving him another chance. He wanted to know whether, as a Christian trying to live by Jesus' general instructions, he had done the right thing.

While his earnestness in running a business by Christian principles made me very proud of him, I chuckled a little. He's been listening to my sermons from the Bible for years, but, like all the rest of us, he wasn't certain exactly what the Scriptures would have him do in this case. The dilemma his crooked employee posed for him presented itself as an excellent test case. "What would the Lord have me do right now?" My years of general teachings weren't enough. He needed direct instruction.

Jesus' directive

So does Peter. "Put out into deep water, and let down the nets for a catch" (Luke 5:4). Jesus turns from the crowd to the individual. One-on-one tutoring has begun. So long as the master was addressing the masses, nothing more was required of Peter than to pilot the boat. Jesus' words flew beyond him to the crowd. Now the time has come for eye contact. Without it, the speaker's words weren't connecting with the hearer's will.

That's how it was at Gate 85 in the San Francisco airport as I waited to board United Airlines' flight 783 to Phoenix. Six people had lined up at the counter. The attendant had something very important to say, but she never once looked at the persons she was talking to, including the first one in line, who was no more than three feet away from her. Instead, she grasped the microphone firmly in her hand, fixed her gaze on something on the floor, and announced through the public address system, "To those

of you who are waiting at the podium, we have just fin-
ished taking care of a departing flight and won't be ready
for the flight to Phoenix for another two-three-four-five
minutes. The flight will be posted when we are ready to
serve you."

With that, she returned the microphone to its cradle,
shifted her focus to the desk, and continued ignoring her
customers. She had made her public address. That she had
communicated personally with no one seemed of no concern to her. The six passengers continued their vigil, hoping that in time the officious nonattendant might actually
talk to them.

Given the popularity of Jesus as a public speaker, we
don't doubt that when he addressed a crowd he made eye
contact. He saw them; they saw him see them, and when
they were beyond his line of vision (as Peter probably was,
sitting beside or behind him as he spoke), he shifted his
gaze until the connection was made. "Put out into deep
water. . . ."

Peter's protest
He may be a brilliant teacher, this Jesus, learned in
Scripture and authoritative in tone—but when it comes to
fishing, well, this is Peter's business. When he was but a
boy his father began teaching him the ropes, and he has
learned well. He knows how to read the signs in the sky,
the currents in the sea, the whimsical comings and goings
of the fish, the care and maintenance of his boats and nets.
And he knows that some days (and nights) the fish just
aren't to be found. You can let down and haul in your nets
until your back is breaking, but if they aren't there they
aren't there. And so help me, they aren't there!

Furthermore, the fishermen are tired. "We've worked
hard all night. . ." (v. 5). The prospect of more fishing, even
if they find the fish, isn't appealing.

A much later disciple of Christ, the Reformation leader

John Calvin, was as reluctant to take up his task as Peter is his. Guillaume Farel was importuning the brilliant but reclusive young scholar to join him in Geneva. Together they would lead the city according to their Protestant understanding of God's will. Calvin was not easily persuaded, pleading his youth and unfitness but mainly his love for study. He was more fit for the quiet of libraries than for shouldering the onerous duties of civic leadership, for which he had no experience. Finally, according to Calvin's biographer, the exasperated Farel rose, extended his hand over Calvin, and scolded, "You have no other pretext for refusing me than the attachment which you declare you have for your studies. But I tell you, in the name of God Almighty, that *if you do not share with me the holy work in which I am engaged he will not bless your plans, because you prefer your repose to Jesus Christ!*" The speech may sound presumptuous to modern ears, but Calvin heard Farel's as the voice of God, and he consented.[2] His protest was over.

Peter's reluctant obedience

So is Peter's. "Because you say so. . ." (v. 5). He is not admitting that Jesus knows what he is doing. As I said, when it comes to catching fish, Peter has the expertise. And it is apparent he's not lazy. Tired though he is ("we've worked hard all night"), he goes to work, along with his fellow fishermen.

Now, if Walt Disney were telling this story, about right here the merry fishermen would begin singing as they worked the oars and the nets, like Snow White's friends traipsing off to the mines every morning happily harmonizing, "Heigh ho, heigh ho, it's off to work we go!" But that wasn't after all night on the job, like Peter and his friends. Their weary bodies make their willing spirits all the more admirable. "Because you say so . . ." isn't the most enthusiastic response they could have given Jesus, but it is enough. (Besides, I've always been a little suspicious of those miners, haven't you?)

When you're worn out, you don't want to do anything that requires energy—even if the Lord tells you to. I admire Peter for doing what he's told, don't you?

The result

In all their years on the lake, the men had never seen anything like this haul. So heavy that it was snapping cords and straining muscles to the limit, the catch was more than they could handle. They had to call for help. (All blessings it seems, even marine ones, are for sharing!)

You can't help thinking of another Scripture, on a completely unrelated subject, that promises incredible returns on some invested faith. In the third chapter of Malachi, the prophet (conveying God's message), charges his people with violating his decrees: "Ever since the time of your forefathers you have turned away from my decrees and have not kept them. Return to me, and I will return to you." He assumes the people won't understand him. "But you ask, 'How are we to return?'" (v. 7).

Not ready to give them a direct answer, he draws out the charge: "Will a man rob God? Yet you rob me" (v. 8).

Again, a rhetorical question, does their speaking for them, "But you ask, 'How do we rob you?'"

Now at last he's ready to complete the case against them: "In tithes and offerings. You are under a curse—the whole nation of you—because you are robbing me" (v. 9).

At this point we preachers like to thunder forth on the principles of stewardship in general and the necessity of tithing in particular. We stress the close relationship between faith in God and obedience to him in everything, including what we do with our money. What interests us right now, though, are the nearly unbelievable rewards to be enjoyed when the nation is faithful in this ongoing discipline of faith:

"Test me in this," says the Lord Almighty, "and see if I will not throw open the floodgates of heaven and pour out so much blessing that you will not have room enough for it. I will prevent pests from devouring your crops, and the vines in your fields will not cast their fruit," says the Lord Almighty. "Then all the nations will call you blessed, for yours will be a delightful land," says the Lord Almighty.   Malachi 3:10-12

Extravagant promises—not enough room for the blessings in Malachi, not strong enough nets for the catch in Luke. (If you think these are isolated instances, remember Matthew 6:25-34, and while you're at it check out Matthew 7:7-11; 13:1-23; 17:20; 21:21, 22. There are many more.)

This was only the first of many surprises ahead for Peter. When you become a disciple of Jesus Christ, you're like the bride and groom who spent their wedding night in the bridal suite of a fancy hotel. The wedding was late and the reception was later, so by the time they arrived at their lodging, the night was nearly spent. Entering their bridal suite, they were surprised to find only a sofa, some chairs, and a table—no bed.

Fortunately, the sofa was a hide-a-bed—but one with soggy springs and a lumpy mattress. They were too tired to protest or demand other accommodations, so they spent a fitful night, greeting the morning with sore backs and bad attitudes. The new husband rose to his responsibilities and marched to the lobby where he accosted the management with as stern a tongue-lashing as he could deliver.

The manager remained calm. "Did you open the door in the room?" he asked.

The husband returned to the room a little less huffily. There he discovered that the door he and his bride thought was a closet was, in fact, the way into a beautifully furnished bedroom, where they also found their complimentary fruit basket and chocolates.

The management had wanted to please. The bride and

groom just hadn't take full advantage of the hospitality.

The results for Peter and his comrades were pleasing in the extreme, once they decided to follow Jesus' order.

That's how the Lord rewards his disciples.

The response

Like the newlyweds, I have upon occasion jumped to some pretty hasty conclusions myself. It's pretty easy for me to identify with Peter. "Go away from me, Lord; I am a sinful man!" (Luke 5:8). Jesus interprets Peter's response as fear: "Don't be afraid. . ." (v. 10). But what's the source of his fear? Luke implies that, because of the enormity of the catch, they have been made aware of a power they haven't seen before; they realize they are in the presence of a personality far stronger than their own. This must be the working of God. Has this man Jesus come from God? Is he, somehow, of God?

Peter's reaction recalls Isaiah's, when he saw the Lord high and lifted up in the temple (Isaiah 6:1-7). "Woe to me!" Isaiah cried. His vision of God made him see himself more clearly, and he hated what he saw: "I am ruined! For I am a man of unclean lips, and I live among a people of unclean lips. . . ."

"Go away from me, Lord," says Peter. You are holy, you are powerful, you can do amazing things. And me? I don't belong in your presence. "I am a sinful man!"

The new priority

Jesus ignores Peter's chagrin, except to put his mind at ease. He doesn't argue with Peter. It's as if he is telling him, "All right, so you're a sinful man. So far that's the only kind I've found around here. We'll take care of that problem later. My Father has a plan for wiping your sin away once and for all, when the time comes. But in the meantime, we have work to do. From now on you will catch men."

You have a new priority, Peter. You've fished for fish, and you've been good at it. I am here, however, to offer you a far more meaningful assignment—one of much greater consequence. You've dedicated your life to fish that swim for a while in the sea and are gone. Now you must devote yourself to human beings who dwell for a while on the land but whom God wants to live with him in eternity.

"So they pulled their boats up on shore, left everything and followed him" (v. 11).

The new priority is theirs.

And it will make all the difference.

---

[1]Copyright 1994 by NEA, Inc.
[2]Edwin Charles Dargan, *A History of Preaching*, Volume 1. Grand Rapids: Baker Book House, 1968, p. 445.

2

What Did I Ever Do to Deserve This?

Blessed are the poor in spirit,
for theirs is the kingdom of heaven.
Matthew 5:3

The first Beatitude takes issue with a very popular, much-encouraged posture, the one that boasts, "I deserve." It assumes many forms, as in the popular lament, "What did I ever do to deserve this?" or any number of persuasive commercials, like, "You deserve a break today at McDonald's" or, "It's expensive, but I'm worth it."

This "I deserve" mantra, promoted as a good exercise in building self-esteem, is as alien in spirit to the first Beatitude as it can be. Jesus reserves his praise for people who acknowledge they *don't* deserve and don't expect to be honored, or coddled, or handed good breaks, or given everything the self-satisfied are convinced should be theirs. The poor in spirit don't demand to be first in line; they don't head for the chief seats. They don't go on strike for more wages than they're worth. This Beatitude decidedly does not "Look Out for Number One." As you can imagine, it's not the most popular of Jesus' sayings, especially to a me-first generation.

There's a further difficulty with it. Matthew's version reads, "poor in spirit," but Luke's doesn't spiritualize Jesus' teaching. "Blessed are you who are poor," he says. Plain and simple—and scary (Luke 6:20). Matthew we can handle; what are we to make of Luke? Who can hear it? What about the rich, or relatively so, like most of us middle-class Christians who own our (mortgaged) homes and drive our own cars (on time payments), luxuries that elevate us high above most of the world's population? Must we become poor, divest ourselves of our possessions, to enjoy the blessing of God? [1]

The Greek word used here would almost lead you to think so. Matthew could have employed *penes*, which expresses the poverty of a person who must work with his hands and provide for his own needs. Instead, Matthew opts for *ptochos*, the word for absolute, abject poverty.

Luke compounds our consternation by quoting Jesus just four verses later: "But woe to you who are rich, for you have already received your comfort" (6:24). Is this Jesus' way of saying, "You've already got what you wanted, what you were so certain you deserved"? (The Roman Emperor, Julian the Apostate [A.D. 332-63] is reputed to have seriously quipped that he wanted to confiscate Christians' property so that they might all become poor and enter the kingdom of Heaven. He took Luke's version seriously.)

Philip Yancey, one of my favorite authors, comes to my rescue here. He credits Monica Hellwig for helping him, as he has helped me (italics mine), to see some of the advantages of being poor, advantages Jesus may well have had in mind in this Beatitude:

- The poor know they are in urgent need of redemption. *(They can't get out of their predicament on their own. They simply don't have the resources. Therefore they aren't too proud to accept rescue.)*
- The poor know not only their dependence on God and on powerful people but also their interdependence with one another. *(To pretend independence would only aggravate their situation. When they cry, "God help me," their prayer is in earnest. When they ask of people who do have resources, or when they turn to the others—family, friends, neighbors, church—they openly admit their powerlessness.)*
- The poor rest their security on people, not things. *(They may dream of ownership someday, but their real hope is in persons who care.)*
- The poor have no exaggerated sense of their own importance and no exaggerated need of privacy. *(Unless you've been really poor, you don't realize what an expensive luxury privacy is.)*
- The poor expect little from competition and much from cooperation. *(When you can't afford to go it alone, you learn to give and take. Sharing saves lives.)*
- The poor can distinguish between necessities and luxuries *(You don't dine on croissants and jam when you can't afford bread and butter.)*
- The poor can wait, because they have acquired a kind of dogged patience born of acknowledged dependence. *(And in their waiting they can see just how time-poor are the money-wealthy.)*

- The fears of the poor are more realistic and less exaggerated, because they already know that one can survive great suffering and want. *(For them, life is real and it is hard. They don't indulge in imagined sufferings.)*

- When the poor have the gospel preached to them, it sounds like good news and not like a scolding. *(It sounds like good news because it really is. Finally they are learning about someone who really understands and cares and can do something about their deepest needs.)*

- The poor can respond to the call of the gospel with a certain abandonment and uncomplicated totality because they have so little to lose and are ready for anything. *(The rich young man who had everything but the one thing Jesus demanded couldn't—because he wouldn't—abandon his holdings. His wealth owned him. For the poor, on the other hand, there's only one way to go, and that's up.)*[2]

I prefer Matthew's version to Luke's, not because I'm not poor, but because I've known some poor who did not fit Yancey's list. They are poor but proud, impoverished but unteachable. Their penury has embittered and isolated them, and in their anger they turn against those who can best help them, even God. They haven't learned the lessons their poverty can teach them. You would not, by the wildest stretch of the imagination, call their state "blessed." Yet I've included the list and my comments because both versions of Jesus' Beatitude demand attention. The Bible is far from silent on the subject of God's special concern for the poor.

To be "poor in spirit," in Matthew's phrase, is to be teachable, open to the leading of the Lord and willing to submit to a Savior's guidance. Some commentators believe this Beatitude to be more than the first among several;

they consider it the base on which all the rest stand, serving like a heading for the others that follow. They have a good argument. If persons lack this fundamental humility, who can teach them? They embody the bluster in William Ernest Henley's famous poem, "Invictus." I wonder whether high school English teachers still assign it. One of mine not only required we study the poem but recommended it as an inspirational work for recharging a discouraged soul. At first reading, its passion seems admirable.

> Out of the night that covers me,
>   Black as the pit from pole to pole,
> I thank whatever gods may be
>   For my unconquerable soul.
>
> In the fell clutch of circumstance
>   I have not winced nor cried aloud.
> Under the bludgeonings of chance
>   My head is bloody, but unbowed.
>
> Beyond this place of wrath and tears
>   Looms but the Horror of the shade,
> And yet the menace of the years
>   Finds and shall find me unafraid.
>
> It matters not how strait the gate,
>   How charged with punishments the scroll,
> I am the master of my fate:
>   I am the captain of my soul.

As I said, it sounds good at first, if you don't think too much about it, but further study bares the futility beneath the bravado. An unconquerable soul may be an asset if a person's fate is decided by a toss of the gods' dice. If your lot is to battle alone in a hostile or indifferent universe, then you'd best take command of your destiny and fight to the death. But if there really is a God, and if he rules by grace and love, then it's absurd to shake your puny fist in his face and boast of your superior might. God has a way of handling such rebels: he lets them have their way.

Blessing awaits the poor in spirit *because* they are willing for God to be God. They'd prefer he be captain of their souls. He's better at the job than they are.

The "poor in spirit" don't strut, don't construct their own empires, don't delight in commanding, don't dictate others' emotions. Having found a worthy master, they are content to follow. They prefer learning to teaching, listening to talking, comforting to being comforted. They would rather see than be seen.

After reading "Invictus," we turn for relief to Philippians 2, where Paul calls for an attitude like that of Jesus:

> *Who, being in very nature God, did not consider equality with God something to be grasped, but made himself nothing, taking the very nature of a servant, being made in human likeness. And being found in appearance as a man, he humbled himself and became obedient to death—even death on a cross!*
>
> *(vv. 6-8)*

This, wouldn't you say, is what it means to be poor in spirit?

John Updike would apply this Beatitude to the writer's craft. The noted novelist warns against the dangers of success. When authors become celebrities, self-consciousness takes over. Their skill depends on their looking with unblurred vision. With success, being seen replaces seeing. They follow their fans' eyes back to themselves. "Celebrity is a mask that eats into the face," he says. "As soon as one is aware of being 'somebody,' to be watched and listened to with extra interest, input ceases, and the performer goes blind and deaf in his over-animation. One can either see or be seen. . . . The 'successful' writer acquires a film over his eyes. His eyes get fat."[3]

Fat-eyed persons, be they writers or preachers or barbers or whatever, would be terribly ill at ease in the *kingdom of Heaven*, where all eyes are on God. Before him, every knee shall bow and every tongue confess that he is Lord. In the crowd thronging the heavenly throne, fat-eyed people would be desperate to get out. No one would be paying any attention to them!

To see this Beatitude in action, with its attending unselfconsciousness, check out John the Baptist. In spite of the popularity of his ministry at the Jordan, John kept his balance. He had come to be a forerunner of the Messiah. His days in the limelight were numbered. When Jesus approached John in order to be baptized, he recognized the man whose fame and influence would soon eclipse his own. He later good-naturedly admitted, "He must become greater; I must become less" (John 3:30).

For people accustomed to being in charge, it seems unnatural at first to step back and let someone else take over. This need to control makes it extremely difficult for some to accept even God's sovereignty in their lives—to let him become greater.

A superb example of this "becoming greater" is the conversion of Zacchaeus (Luke 19:1-10). As far as we know, the tax collector already enjoyed good health and lots of wealth when Jesus spied him in the sycamore-fig tree. He may have even protested that he had been obeying God and, according to his lights, living right. By every material standard, God had treated him right. He raked in profits from the most notorious of professions. He wasn't satisfied, though. Would a complacent man have felt compelled, when Jesus came into his life, to disperse half his holdings and to repay by four times anyone he had cheated? Zacchaeus had found something (someone?) far more satisfying than money. Suddenly he felt the need to rearrange his priorities. He who had chased wealth would now follow Jesus.

His is not an unusual experience, especially among men

and women in midlife. Scarcely a month goes by that someone doesn't seek an appointment for some career counseling. The scripts of these interviews are almost identical:

"All my life I've been working to make money to buy things for myself and my family. I need a change. But I don't want to change to another job or career like the one I've got. I want to do something that makes a difference. I want some kind of ministry, where I am helping people. I want to serve the Lord." The tears are similar also. They can't talk about this strong, overwhelming desire with dry eyes. Zacchaeus's midlife conversion leads him from dissatisfaction to liberation to peace with God in his new home in the kingdom of God.

First comes the dissatisfaction

The much-discussed midlife crisis may take many forms, but the root of the restlessness is the soul's dissatisfaction: "I don't like what I'm doing." "I'm scared my future may be nothing but more of the present." "I don't like what life has done to me." Worst of all, "I don't like the person I've become." Like Zacchaeus seeking out Jesus, don't you think?

You can't always tell by appearances who's hurting. Looking at people's careers and houses and cars and country clubs, you might conclude they have arrived. You're impressed. They aren't, though. These are all just *things*, and they don't satisfy the soul's deepest longings. These people have bought the latest electronic gadgets and seen the right movies and taken their exotic vacations. Still they hunger for more—or rather, for different.

Active seeking

Zacchaeus scrambles up the sycamore tree like a midlifer who has finally decided to do something about his discontent. He wants a better view of this Jesus, about whom he has heard some remarkable, even unbelievable, stories. Is it possible that this man really does have the answer to life's largest questions?

Ambrose Bierce once defined a Christian as one who follows Christ's teachings insofar as they are not incompatible with a life of sin. Could Zacchaeus have had any premonition that Jesus would not only come to his house but would become its master? Could he have guessed that changing his priorities would cost him so dearly?

The risk in looking for something different is that you may find it.

Actively being sought

Zacchaeus must have been as surprised as the crowd when Jesus invited himself to the tax collector's home. "Zacchaeus, come down immediately. I must stay at your house today." The seeker is being sought!

There's nothing peculiar about Zacchaeus's experience. Believers who have found Christ in midlife discover that he had been waiting for them all along, looking for a sign that they were ready. Others who have been lifelong disciples testify that somewhere in midlife they discovered in reviewing their lives that the Lord has been guiding all along, even when they thought the were making independent decisions. It is as if, in the words of Mother Teresa's prayer, "May Jesus use you without consulting you," he has been using them all along, without asking. The Lord is passive in our lives only at our request.

His actions often surprise. Listen to the muttering of the onlookers. They never quite know what to make of Jesus. They are astonished that this rabbi, if that's what he is, would enter a "sinner's" house. This is not how a truly holy man would behave.

Zacchaeus doesn't object. He is grateful. More than grateful, overcome. "Lord," he called Jesus. And Lord he became.

Payback time

Zacchaeus seems to come to the decision on his own. He can't have a fresh future without settling past debts. He will right the wrongs he has done. He will reach out to the poor he has ignored. He will put into practice what he is learning about the will of God. He will bring order and unity into his life. He will seek first the kingdom of God, he who has sought first the lining of his pockets.

I'm intrigued that he says nothing of giving up his career. Will he continue as a tax collector, that most hated of professions? No one who cared about his reputation would have anything to do with a tax collector, because "everyone" knew they were thieves and cheats and a disgrace to their nation.

My guess is that Zacchaeus went right back to his tax table, but now as an honest broker. He has become a disciple of Jesus first and foremost; he will practice his discipleship under difficult circumstances. Zacchaeus used to be a tax collector; now he is a disciple of Jesus who happens to be a tax collector. There's a big difference.

Welcome home! "Today salvation has come. . . ."

You're where you belong, Zacchaeus, becoming the person God intended you to be. You can now grasp what another disciple of Jesus, Paul, will write several decades later. Comparing all the advantages he enjoyed as a religious leader in his pre-Christian life with what he now experiences as a Christian, he concludes:

> *But whatever was to my profit I now consider loss for the sake of Christ. What is more, I consider everything a loss compared to the surpassing greatness of knowing Christ Jesus my Lord, for whose sake I have lost all things. I consider them rubbish, that I may gain Christ.*   Philippians 3:7, 8

Zacchaeus *has* gained Christ. Destination achieved. Blessing received.

[1]See, for example, Mark 10:17-31.

[2]Philip Yancey, "The Peculiar Blessings of Poverty," *Christianity Today*, June 16, 1989, p. 72.

[3]John Updike, *Self-Consciousness*. New York: Alfred A. Knopf, 1989, p. 252.

3

A Time to Mourn, a Time to Laugh

Blessed are those who mourn,
for they will be comforted.
Matthew 5:4

Just before the first service one Sunday, Dr. Terry Wood called me aside. He had a story too good to keep to himself. A few days earlier Terry's wife, Candy, was attempting to explain the death of Terry's father to their four-year-old son, Andrew. "We can't see Grandpa Cookie now," she said, "because he's died and gone to Heaven to be with God and now he's playing with the angels."

Andrew wasn't buying her story. He knew better. "The Angels play in California," he corrected her.

The second Beatitude was pretty hard for me to buy too, for a long time. It made no sense. Mourning and

blessing did not belong together. After several years of
pastoral ministry, though, I considered the alternative:
"Blessed are those who *don't* or *can't* mourn." No, the
hard-hearted or incapacitated are not blessed. They are
deprived.

As I write these words, my ninety-year-old mother still
languishes in her nursing home. More than fifteen years
ago we detected the first hints of her Alzheimer's Syn-
drome—the little forgetfulnesses, the periodic confusion,
the fear of going anyplace new, the inability to name the
family members whose pictures adorned her walls.
Slowly, inexorably, she slipped deeper into the darkness
until at last there was no calling her back. If she hears us
now or understands what we say to her, it's her secret. She
offers no response, gives us no sign that she is receiving
our love. Her vital signs remain strong. She eats and
processes her food, but beyond these simple mechanical
activities—nothing.

My mother can't mourn.

Hers is an extreme example, admittedly, but not a rare
one. In Mother's nursing home, just one of thousands like
it, are dozens of men and women who have lost their ability to love, to talk, to laugh, and to mourn. Old age has
ravaged them.

Equally heartbreaking are the war-ravaged. Nations
mourn the loss of their young men and women on the
fields of battle. But on every battlefield there are soldiers
so war-weary, who have lost so much, that they have
become numb to the carnage around them. They can't feel
anymore. As American poet John Peale Bishop once wrote,
"The most tragic thing about the war was not that it made
so many dead men, but that it destroyed the tragedy of
death." Life was cheapened, senses were dulled, and
everyone was victimized. They couldn't mourn.

The gruesome fact is that the ability to mourn is not a
universal human trait. I've just mentioned the aged and

those victimized by war. We could borrow the jargon of medicine and social science and add sociopaths, psychopaths, schizophrenics, autistic and other mentally disabled persons whose alienation from other human beings makes us wonder whether they do or can mourn. If not, we don't envy their immunity.

Jesus has got it right. Blessed are those who mourn.

No stranger to mourning

Mourning was a subject Jesus' contemporaries knew a lot about. Life expectancy in the first century was probably no longer than twenty years or so. It rose significantly only in the nineteenth and twentieth centuries, when medical science scored breakthroughs in combating mass epidemics, reducing infant mortality, and preventing mothers' deaths in childbirth. A baby born today can anticipate living to nearly eighty years of age; by the late 1800s our great-great grandparents could expect an average of only about thirty-four years.

To Jesus' first century audience, then, mourning was a frequent experience. The spirit of resignation that permeates Ecclesiastes resonated with their experience. Life was hard, death was frequent.

> *There is a time for everything,*
> *and a season for every activity under heaven:*
> *a time to be born and a time to die,*
> *a time to plant and a time to uproot, . . .*
> *a time to weep and a time to laugh,*
> *a time to mourn and a time to dance.*
>
> *Ecclesiastes 3:1, 2, 4*

Once again Luke records Jesus' words slightly differently than Matthew does. "Blessed are you who weep now, for you will laugh" (Luke 6:21). And once more he adds a warning missing in Matthew's version: "Woe to you who laugh now, for you will mourn and weep" (6:25).

Luke captures the balance of Ecclesiastes. Jesus appears to be talking less about divine retribution in the coming judgment day than he is about the normal, observable flux of everyday life with its maddening mix of good and bad news. "Be patient," he comforts the bereaved, "your status will change." "Be warned," he admonishes the frivolous, "your turn is coming."

In Matthew, however, Jesus seems to be speaking of receiving comfort *while* mourning. To all who have lost loved ones, this is good news indeed. We aren't pining to dance again; we are grateful for much less. Just a little comfort as we weep. We don't expect our sense of loss ever to leave us completely. In truth, we don't want it to. It would disappear only if we could forget our loved one, and that's a price we are unwilling to pay. We will return to our old routines, but we will never be quite our old selves. From time to time, the memories will flood and the tears will overflow.

For us the blessing must come even as our mourning quietly continues; we're not going to "get over" the loss of our beloved.

A group of volunteers were on the Pacific Christian College campus recently; they come every year to donate their labor in our ongoing project of beautifying the campus. They are cherished friends. After a hard day of painting, pounding, and scrubbing, they rested most evenings by going for their evening walk—to get their exercise! I went along one evening for the fellowship. Barbara and I soon separated ourselves from the others, so we could talk. It had been almost a year since she and her husband, Mo, had lost their thirty-five-year-old son to a fatal illness, leaving a stunned wife and two-year-old child. "Will it ever get easier?" Barbara asked. She was embarrassed that she still grieved so strongly after so many months, yet the pain wouldn't go away.

"Yes," I could assure her, "it will get easier. But you'll

never get over it entirely. You don't want to. You cherish the memories, and whether they are summoned or arrive unbidden, their coming renews the longing, the hurt. But you would not give up remembering for anything. In a sense, we invite the pain." My words were probably not very comforting, but they were honest, born of personal experience. I read somewhere of a doctor who considered that grieving that extended more than a year was pathological. How wrong experts can be. Like Barbara, people who have loved deeply will remember and cry, but they will carry on, grateful for the memories and the Lord's promised comfort, which they do receive even in their mourning.

Mourning comes to the bereaved

Rabbi Earl Grollman, of Toronto, tells of the time he and his brother, also a rabbi, went to the mortuary after the death of their mother. The funeral director was impressed by his distinguished visitors. It wasn't often he had two rabbis present, he told them. He meant his words as flattery, but he misread the men. They weren't there as rabbis, the brothers enlightened him, but as grieving sons. Even professional clergymen have feelings. I can't tell you the number of visits I've made to funeral homes during my forty years of ministry, When I have gone after the death of a parent, a dear friend, or my son, my "profession" was the last thing I was thinking of. I went as a person, wept as a lover, and received the embraces of comforters with wordless gratitude.

Dr. Diane Komp, a pediatrician specializing in childhood cancer, has also seen a great deal of mourning up close. She recalls a father who had lost three children in early infancy to the same disease. His religious faith was not much solace to him, believing, as he told her, that "God was more than passively involved in their suffering as a family." Dr. Komp considers his belief about God's

culpability more painful than unbelief would be. In spite
of his anguish, though, when they lost their fourth child,
he and his wife "postponed their own grief to organize the
medical staff of a small community hospital. Thanks to
them, blood samples, placenta, and autopsy material were
preserved for a research team in a distant state. They facili-
tated a breakthrough in the understanding of the disease
that will benefit children and parents of the future, but not
them directly."[1] Dr. Komp adds, "This couple may have
lacked answers as to *why*, but they understood *what* action
their faith required of them."

I retold Dr. Komp's story to get to that final sentence.
Mourning almost always raises unwelcome questions and
doubts. Everyone knows that comfort comes most readily
to those who feel closest to God. The courage of these parents and others like them who have lost children to cancer
makes Dr. Komp recall J. B. Phillips's rendering of 2 Corinthians 4:9: "We may be knocked down but we are never
knocked out!" But even someone like this four-times-
bereaved father, whose suspicion that God took an active
part in the deaths of his children must have driven him to
the brink of madness, found a positive way to ease his
anguish. He and his wife were knocked down but not
knocked out. They got up to serve. In their serving they
found comfort.

This couple remind me of Dr. John and Mabel Ross.
John was ordained into the Christian ministry by the same
preacher who presided at my ordination, so I followed his
career with more than casual interest. When he and Mabel
buried their fourth child, they knew what they had to do.
John resigned from his church, enrolled in medical school,
and devoted the rest of his life to the practice of medicine,
first in Africa and then, when his Parkinson's disease
brought him back to America, on an Indian reservation in
Southern California. He and Mabel were down but not
out. They got up to serve, and found comfort.

Mourning comes to the divorced

While I was writing this chapter, a good friend has been on my mind. He's a successful businessman in his sixties. His first marriage produced six children, of whom he is inordinately proud. Their mother, he is the first to tell you, was excellent, but the marriage didn't last. He then married again, but after just a few years that relationship soured, also. When I visited him not long ago and asked how he was doing, he was as candid as always. "I'm miserable," he told me. We spent several hours together. How I wished I could have waved a magic wand to heal the hurt and restore the marriage. He is in mourning for a dead relationship.

Friends who have experienced both the death of a loved one and a divorce report that death is easier. Sometimes the grieving over divorce lasts years. Even when it's over life isn't the same.

When, then, does the comfort come? It comes when you are ready for it. If you've been divorced, a counselor probably would outline something like the following steps for your recovery:

- First, face the facts. *The marriage is over. You can't relive yesterday.*
- Then own up to your share of the responsibility. *Casting all the blame on your former spouse only compounds your problems. If you give way to anger and bitterness, you warp your own personality and endanger your health. You, not your former spouse, are the loser.*
- Believe God's promises and count on his providence. *Your divorce is a disappointment to him, admittedly, but he is not ready to cast you out of his presence. Let him help.*
- But don't expect him to do everything. *You are now ready for a fresh start, one that builds on the lessons you've learned the hard way.*

- Say good-bye to your days as critic and judge of others. *You now have a new sympathy, a deeper understanding, a warmer heart.*
- Don't rush into the arms of someone else. *You've been damaged. You need time to heal and to gain insight into yourself. You don't want to make the same mistakes again.*

Mourning comes to the estranged

Death and divorce are the obvious causes of mourning. Not so apparent, but equally real and painful, is the ending of a close relationship. When a friendship is betrayed, or a trusted business partnership turns sour, or a permanent move to a faraway place separates dear ones, it's time to weep. Such breaches in former relationships are to be expected, unfortunately. But some people seem to recover much quicker than others. How do they do it?

David Reagan, who travels the country speaking on prophecy and end times, studied this question up close one evening. He was visiting in an elder's home following a Sunday evening service, when the phone rang at about 10:30. Dr. Reagan heard his host exclaim, "Oh no! Oh no!" The two men immediately drove to the hospital, the elder explaining they were on their way to see a young woman Dr. Reagan had just met that evening at church. She had hurried away from the service to open the skating rink for a group of the church's young people. Later, she had been skating with them when she suddenly dropped to the floor. Only thirty-two, she had suffered a massive cerebral hemorrhage. A large group of youngsters and friends from the church filled the hospital lobby and hallway, praying, singing softly, comforting one another. Then the doctor came with the bad news. She had died instantly.

Her older sister received the news calmly, consoling the others, reminding them of the young woman's faith in the Lord, to whom she had gone. Then her brother arrived. A man of the world, he had scoffed at the woman's faith, but grief and guilt overcame him now. He wept and moaned loudly. His sister offered no pity. "Don't weep for your sister. Weep for yourself. She's in Heaven with the Lord. But if that were you in there on that table, you would be in Hell." Reagan was startled by her boldness, but within a year her brother had accepted the Lord.

While Dr. Reagan moved from group to group comforting and praying, two paramedics suddenly ran in pushing a gurney toward the emergency room. On the stretcher was an older man, perhaps sixty, dressed in a tuxedo. Soon a large crowd of "beautiful people" assembled. They had been partying at a night club, where the man collapsed on the dance floor. Heart attack, they thought.

They were right. More bad news from the doctor. The patient had died. Reagan was unprepared for what happened next. These "beautiful people" stood for a moment in a daze, then attacked each other "like a pack of wild animals." The man's daughter turned on her mother. "It's all your fault. You're the cause of his heart attack. You've never given him anything but grief," she accused her mother.

"Look who's talking," the mother shouted back, "the biggest slut in southern Louisiana."

Dr. Reagan marveled at the contrast as he stood between the two groups. In one, people were hugging each other, praying together, offering whatever comfort they could. In the other, imprecations and accusations separated one from another. Hebrews 2:15 came to his mind, which says that Jesus died that He might "free those who all their lives were held in slavery by their fear of death." He also thought of Revelation 14:13, "Blessed are the dead who die in the Lord."[2]

Both groups grieved, but how much greater is the hurt when relationships are strained. Where love is, mourners draw close to and comfort one another; where love is not, mourning separates and embitters.

Mourning comes when hope dies

When Medford Jones told me he was being tested for lymphoma, my heart sank. Medford has been my friend since we first met in 1957, a predecessor in the presidency of Pacific Christian College, a challenging verbal sparring partner, and always a trusted confidant. Then when the diagnosis was confirmed, my earlier foreboding turned to grieving. At his age (seventy-seven), I was convinced the prognosis would be bleak. He was alive and very actively contributing to the college, but my mourning had begun.[3]

This was not the first time mourning began at the prospect, not the reality, of death. When our son, Lane, took his life at twenty-six, Joy and I felt the full force of the blow. Friends commented as time went on, though, about how well we seemed to be recovering. We appeared stronger than we felt, apparently. If we were in fact coming back to life more quickly than others expected, we knew why. As Joy explained it, we had begun our grieving years earlier. Lane's battle with his health had been going on since he was eight. We had helped him through his mood swings, counseled him on his diet, encouraged him in his moves to find a friendlier environment, read the signs of his growing discouragement, prayed that the Lord would heal his body, and steeled ourselves for what we were afraid might happen. When it did happen, we were dismayed, but not completely surprised.

For Lane himself, we aren't certain exactly when his hope died. He had seriously considered suicide once before, we knew, but had rejected it out of deference to his family. When at last he had exhausted his resources, his hope gave out. And so did he.

When hope dies, mourning begins.

Mourning comes
when love grieves for the lost

The New Testament speaks of grieving for those who show no repentance. Paul writes in 2 Corinthians 12:21, "I am afraid that when I come again my God will humble me before you, and I will be grieved over many who have sinned earlier and have not repented of the impurity, sexual sin and debauchery in which they have indulged." Paul's heartache resonates with that of Jesus, whose ministry began with his cry from the depths. His mission was to rescue the lost sheep of Israel, but their fate was in their hands. He could deliver them only if they let him. He urgently begged them, "The time has come. The kingdom of God is near. Repent and believe the good news!" (Mark 1:15). The news *was* good—but their condition was deplorable. The nearness of the kingdom would be cause for rejoicing, provided they wept first.

There is a disappointment so profound it feels like mourning. For Paul, the unrepentant are like the living dead, for unless they turn their lives back to God, there is no hope for them. He looks to their future and sees only death. His mourning for them has begun.

In 1 Corinthians 5:1, 2 Paul commends grieving for the lost purity of the church:

> It is actually reported that there is sexual immorality among you, and of a kind that does not occur even among pagans: A man has his father's wife. And you are proud! Shouldn't you rather have been filled with grief and have put out of your fellowship the man who did this?

Some mourning is, as Charlie Brown would say, good grief.

For they will be comforted

The promise is certain. You can cast all your anxiety on him, because "he cares for you," as 1 Peter 5:7 reveals.

Therefore those who mourn "will be comforted."
- They will give thanks that they *can* mourn.
- They will welcome the embrace of those who want to love them through their loss.
- They will be able, when another's turn comes, to comfort as they have been comforted.
- They will be told their friends are praying for them, and trust they are.
- They will pray, and know they are heard.
- They will experience God's grace as only the admittedly undeserving can.
- Their hope will be renewed.
- They will laugh again.

---

[1]Diane M. Komp, *A Window to Heaven.* Grand Rapids: Zondervan Publishing House, 1992, p. 117.

[2]Dr. David R. Reagan, *Trusting God.* Shreveport, Louisiana: Huntington House, 1987, pp. 163-165.

[3]Quite prematurely, as it turned out. Medford responded well to his chemotherapy. His doctor assures him that something else will be the cause of his death one day, but not the cancer.

4

Blessed Are
the Debonair

Blessed are the meek, for they
shall inherit the earth.
Matthew 5:5

I hope he was right. Dr. Ian Pitt-Watson, professor of
preaching at Fuller Theological Seminary, once addressed
this text in a sermon. If I had heard him when I was
young, I wouldn't have put up such a fight against Jesus'
third Beatitude, "Blessed are the meek." The meek? The
weak? The wimpy? The nerds?

No, that's not what Jesus meant, Pitt-Watson insisted.
He turned for ammunition to, of all places, a French Bible.
There he discovered the Greek word *praos,* which we
translate into English as *meek,* rendered as *de bon aire* (of
good family or nature). Yes, that's our *debonair,* with its

overtones of gallantry, etiquette, courtesy, and modesty. In the romance literature of the Middle Ages, its incarnation was the knight in shining armor who pledged his gallantry in service to his lady. For her sake he was brave and daring, but he was also gentle and sensitive. He loved life. He was good company. And he was noble. His devotion to his mission tamed his wilder impulses.

"Tamed." That's the key word here.

It's the word that came to mind last summer when Joy and I and our "adopted" kids Jeff and Joan Terrill spent several delightful hours visiting Mont and Elaine Smith in Camus, Washington. The Smith estate is about twenty-five acres of mountain woods that abut national forest land. They live in a natural paradise. There, in a pole barn of his own constructing, Mont stables four of the most beautiful Arabians I've ever seen.

I fell in love. We took two treks so all six of us could ride. Mont courteously gave me his own horse. Accustomed to leading, Princess was obedient but restless in our assigned spot at the end of the train. After awhile, when he saw I knew what I was doing, he said, "Let her go, Roy." So Princess and I broke loose from the pack and I gave her her rein—and held on for one of the most exhilarating rides I've ever had. She tore through the forest, dodging limbs, jumping fallen branches, scrambling surefootedly uphill and down. I confess I thought of Christopher Reeve's paralyzing fall from his horse as I made myself into as small a target as possible for the jutting tree limbs.

On our ride, we came upon a logging road that had been cut through the forest. This time Mont proposed a race. I gladly accepted—and won. I can't take any credit, of course. I was on his horse and had the weight advantage. But again I was startled by the sudden burst of power beneath me; Princess wasn't about to let anyone stay in front of her. She still seemed to be accelerating when we rounded a bend and faced the road's dead end. For an instant I wondered whether we could stop in time. We did.

When she wasn't running, Princess was the calmest, gentlest, easiest-handling horse you could imagine. A quiet word, a gentle touch of the rein against her neck, that's all it took. Her bridle didn't have a bit in it. It wasn't necessary. When we returned to the barn, she went directly into her stall and stood there placidly while I removed her saddle and bridle. She was the meekest of animals. She was, if you please, debonair.

Princess was not at all like those Sons of Thunder, James and John. That was Jesus' nickname for the two ambitious brothers in his disciple band. No wonder. "Teacher, we want you to do for us whatever we ask," they pleaded.[1] Cheeky fellows. What did they want? Only the chief seats in his kingdom—one the Prime Minister and the other Chancellor of the Exchequer—just to be able to lord it over everyone else! Lord Chesterfield once observed of their kind, "Young men are apt to think themselves wise enough, as drunken men are apt to think themselves sober enough." More than one frustrated parent can identify with the father who ran an ad in the classified section of a newspaper: "Complete set of encyclopedias for sale, never used, teen-age son knows everything." It had been owned, perhaps, by James and John.

They are good models of what Jesus does *not* have in mind when speaking of the blessedness of meekness. They have some things to learn.

Meekness is about following, not leading

James and John are young men in a hurry. They've taken the measure of their fellow disciples and like what they have found; they're the best of the lot. They're the most qualified to lead the others. There's another potential leader in the group, that's true. Simon Peter. He usually

dominates discussions and is quick and decisive in tight
situations. But what Peter has in boldness he lacks in judgment. His impulsiveness could lead to trouble. You'd be
better off choosing us, Jesus.

As a class, politicians are not exactly known for their
meekness either. James and John's latter-day counterpart
was Lyndon Johnson, whose political ambition was legendary. Senator John F. Kennedy took advantage of Johnson's reputation at Washington's annual Gridiron Dinner
on March 15, 1958 when he told this story:

"I dreamed about 1960 the other night, and I told Stuart
Symington and Lyndon Johnson about it yesterday. I told
them how the Lord came into my bedroom, anointed my
head, and said, 'John Kennedy, I hereby anoint you President of the United States.' Stu Symington said, 'That's
strange, Jack, because I had a similar dream last night, in
which the Lord anointed me President of the United States
and outer space.' Then Lyndon Johnson said, 'That's very
interesting gentlemen, because I, too, had a similar dream
last night—and I don't remember anointing either one of
you!'"

The joke was funny when Kennedy told it. The megalo-
mania on which it was based became less than humorous
when Johnson was in office fashioning the Great Society,
waging the Vietnam War, trying to be the everyone's
superhero, and getting himself drummed out of office. If
only he had had even a touch of that saving grace, meekness, or had heeded Otto von Bismarck, the great nineteenth-century Prussian statesman, who concluded, "The
best a statesman can do is to listen to the rustle of God's
mantle through history and try to catch the hem of it for a
few steps." The meek listen to, but they don't play, God.

Contrast Johnson if you will with one of science's greatest personalities, Isaac Newton. The brilliant physicist
appraised himself in the humblest of terms: "I do not
know what I may appear to the world; but to myself I

seem to have been only like a boy playing on the seashore, and diverting myself in now and then finding a smoother pebble or a prettier shell than ordinary, whilst the great ocean of truth lay all undiscovered before me."

Even in the sciences, blessed are the meek.

Meekness knows what it doesn't know

"You don't know what you are asking," Jesus tells the importunate brothers. Their ignorance is obvious to the Lord; they are blind to it.

- They don't understand the nature of the kingdom Jesus is establishing.
- They don't know the requirements of the jobs they're volunteering for.
- They don't see the suffering that lies ahead for Jesus and his band.
- They don't sense how offensive their request is to their fellows.
- They don't have the power to see themselves as others see them.
- They lack a saving sense of the ridiculous. They should be laughing at themselves.
- They haven't learned that meekness is more listening, less talking. It is being humble enough to believe that someone else may be right.

Self-promoters like James and John don't know what they don't know. Dr. Lewis Thomas did, though. Among this century's most famous physicians, Dr. Thomas addressed his medical class fifty years after their graduation. He spoke with the wisdom of a man who has learned what he doesn't know.

Almost precisely fifty years ago, all of us passed a milestone in our intellectual development. Within my own memory it was more than a milestone; it was a monument of achievement. You will all remember it, even though it lasted for only a brief period, the span of

time between the final examinations and the first weeks
of internship. It was the best of all possible times in our
lives, the moment when we knew absolutely everything about everything. And, for most of us, certainly
for me, it was the last moment of its kind in a professional lifetime.

Ever since, it has been one confusing ignorance after
another, fifty years of knowing less and less about more
and more, a full half century of advancing bewilder-
ment about medicine, about disease mechanisms, about
human society, about the economics of medicine, and a
mixture of confusion and irritation.[2]

Dr. Thomas belongs in the company of Benjamin
Franklin, who reflected in old age, "I have experienced
many instances of being obliged by better information or
fuller consideration, to change opinions, even on important subjects, which I once thought right, but found to be
otherwise. It is therefore that the older I grow, the more
apt I am to doubt my own judgment, and to pay more
respect to the judgment of others." He describes the
essence of meekness.

This willingness to change, to be taught, to follow the
lead of others, is not necessarily a characteristic of old
age, although Drs. Thomas and Franklin might lead you
to think so. The more common stereotype of old age
employs words like stubborn, crotchety, rigid, and brittle.
Years ago I ran across these lines by Lao-tzu worth
remembering:

> Humans are born soft and supple;
> dead, they are stiff and hard.
> Plants are born tender and pliant;
> dead, they are brittle and dry.
>
> Thus whoever is stiff and inflexible
> is a disciple of death.
> Whoever is soft and yielding
> Is a disciple of life.

Meekness is about life. It knows that it doesn't know enough—and wants to learn more.

Meekness waits on God's timing for both assignment and reward

The meek can wait with patience until God chooses to call them. In the meantime, they work. "Can you drink the cup?" Jesus isn't toying with James and John. He sees the danger ahead. He wants them to prepare for the hardships before them.

Even after they protest their readiness, he can't give what they want. Their promotion "is not for me to grant," he tells them. "These places belong to those for whom they have been prepared." Jesus himself must submit to the Father's sovereignty.

What, then, are James and John to do in the meantime? Just what you and I must do. The real question is never, "Lord, will you give us what we want?" but rather, "Lord, what needs to be done now? What would you have us do here, today?"

And in the meantime, we wait to see what the Lord has prepared for us, content to sit at the table or serve it. We adopt the attitude of Paul, who learned:

> *to be content whatever the circumstances. I know what it is to be in need, and I know what it is to have plenty. I have learned the secret of being content in any and every situation, whether well fed or hungry, whether living in plenty or in want. I can do everything through him who gives me strength.*
>
> *Philippians 4:11-13*

He would serve wherever God placed him. He would be content. We call his attitude meekness.

Meekness climbs up by going down

James and John have to learn the lesson required of all Christians. Leadership in the kingdom of God is hyphen-

ated. It is *servant*-leadership. When you have time, check
in a good Bible concordance for the number of times *leadership* appears; then do the same for the word *servant* or
service. You may be surprised.

I think about this often, because the college I serve is a
"leadership training" institution. Our assignment is to prepare men and women to *lead* churches and communities.
The word is deceiving, even distorting, if we teach that a
Christian leader is anything but a servant of the Lord.
There is no job too humble, no task too dirty, for Christian
servants.

James and John are eager to bypass this requirement.
They want to climb the ladder to executive authority
straightaway; no menial service for them. They are so anxious to get to the top they don't care how many others
they step on along the way. In this respect, they are like
the Greeks of their day, who generally considered meekness a vice. They equated it with servility. What would
they have thought of a king who "comes to you, gentle
and riding on a donkey" (Matthew 21:5)? No wonder
James and John's fellow disciples are indignant.

The brothers could have learned a lesson from Georgia's Andrew Young. For several years I have followed his
career with interest and no little admiration. Young
attained national prominence as a young man struggling
beside Martin Luther King in the civil rights movement of
the 1960s. Eventually he served in the United States Congress and then was appointed America's Ambassador to
the United Nations. In every position he distinguished
himself. When he returned home to Atlanta, he attended a
citizens meeting on the future of Atlanta. He went simply
as a citizen; he held no office.

Mayor Maynard Jackson, barred by law from seeking a
third term, delivered a speech analyzing Atlanta's political
and economic situation. Then Mrs. Susie Labond, president of the Public Housing Tenants Association, taking the

floor turned to Mr. Young and challenged him. "Andy," she said, "when you came to Atlanta you wasn't nobody. We took you in and made you somebody. We sent you to Congress, you been Ambassador to the UN, but now we need you to be mayor. If you ain't learned enough to help us, can't nobody help us, and Lord knows we sho need help right now."[3]

Young meekly obeyed the call, and once again served with distinction. Served. His fellow African-American, Cornel West, using *humility* for our word *meekness*, calls humility "the fruit of inner security and wise maturity. To be humble is to be so sure of one's self and one's mission that one can forgo calling excessive attention to one's self and status."[4] When you are that certain of who you are, you can serve at the top or the bottom of the ladder—with distinction.

The Christian life is about serving, not lording

You know that the rulers of the Gentiles lord it over them, and their high officials exercise authority over them. Not so with you. Instead, whoever wants to become great among you must be your servant, and whoever wants to be first must be your slave—just as the Son of Man did not come to be served, but to serve, and to give is life as a ransom for many.

Matthew 20:25-28

Throughout this chapter the best example we know of meekness has inspired every section. No one would accuse Jesus of being weak, or ineffective, or lacking in leadership skills. Eschewing all the perks of high office, he simply did the job his father had sent him to do.

Someone recently gave me a cartoon picturing three overstuffed businessmen at their private, linen-draped, candlelit dining table in an elegant restaurant. The very satisfied host has given his credit card to the tuxedoed waiter who holds it up, smiles, and exclaims, "Ah, not

merely a gold card but a gold card first class with oak-leaf
cluster. How refreshing!" One guest scowls, the other
looks dismayed, the host beams. His status symbol has
trumped any of theirs, no doubt. In your mind's eye, try
putting Jesus at the table. He'd be neither scowling, looking dismayed, nor beaming. He might be pitying, though,
anyone who'd take this or any other status symbol seriously.

As far as Jesus is concerned, "the meek shall inherit the
earth."[5] They already have, you know. Of all living creatures since the earth was created, which ones are now
missing? The great ones: the dinosaurs, the mammoths,
the saber-toothed tigers. And which are still here, doing as
they please, defying every attempt to exterminate them?
The ants, the rats, the amoebas, the meekest of the animal
kingdom. If you don't believe me, please give me your
recipe for getting rid of roaches.

How can we best serve?

Since becoming president of Pacific Christian College in
1990, I have appreciated the third Beatitude more than
ever. Ours is not one of the prestigious institutions of
higher education, at least as the world measures such
things. We aren't a Harvard or Stanford. In academic circles, we couldn't presume to lord it over anyone. Yet we
go about our business without an inferiority complex. We
don't worry about not being in Yale's league, because
that's not our calling. We have a mission. We are to prepare servant-leaders for the church and society. We are to
help churches in their task of discipling the nations. As an
institution we are called to serve. We don't fret over how
we can imitate Oberlin. We ask, rather, how can we fulfill
the calling God has given us? How can we best serve?

Where are *we* needed?

This spirit of servant-leadership has been beautifully
captured by Max DePree, to whom we'll give the final

word in this chapter. One of America's outstanding Christian businessmen, he led the innovative Herman Miller Company as CEO for many years. I first learned of him when he was chairman of the Board of Trustees at Fuller Theological Seminary. He was speaking to a group of college presidents and board chairmen on the subject of leadership. I listened keenly, because few other men had earned the right to teach us on this topic as well as he had, having modeled and written as a proven leader in both business and church circles. When he summarizes the leader's role, his emphasis is not on power or position, but on service. "The first task of a leader is to define reality," he says. "The last task is to say, 'Thank you,' and in between he's a servant." Does anything more need to be said?

James and John, are you listening?

[1]I'm following Mark's version of the story (10:35-45). In Matthew 20:20-28 their mother does the asking.
[2]Reprinted with the permission of Scribner, a Division of Simon & Schuster from THE FRAGILE SPECIES by Lewis Thomas. Copyright © 1992 by Lewis Thomas.
[3]Andrew Young, *A Way Out of No Way, the Spiritual Memoirs of Andrew Young.* Nashville: Thomas Nelson Publishers, 1994, p. 141.
[4]Cornel West, *Race Matters.* Boston: Beacon Press, 1993, pp. 38, 39.
[5]See also Psalm 37:9, 11, 29.

5

The Diet for Building Character Muscles

Blessed are those who hunger and thirst
for righteousness, for they will be filled.
Matthew 5:6

For nearly a year America stared at the television set, mesmerized by O. J. Simpson's first trial. Had he murdered Nicole Brown Simpson and Ron Goldman or not? Would we ever know the truth? No sooner had the trial begun than it became apparent that justice was not what this courtroom drama was all about. It quickly degenerated into a contest between races. Defense Attorney Johnny Cochran skillfully persuaded the jury that racism was the real issue at stake. As the case moved toward its climax, Christopher Darden, one of the prosecuting attorneys, couldn't take any more. "Everybody who has to sit or witness these proceedings, or listen to the details of this crime or these accusations, we're all tarnished," he told the *Los Angeles Times.* "I don't know if I ever want to try another case. . . . It has shaken my faith in a system. . . . Frankly, I'm ashamed to be part of this case."

Sometime after the trial I read his *In Contempt,* which relates a lamentable tale of corruption, deception, and courtroom duplicity. Thoroughly convinced of Simpson's guilt himself, he couldn't persuade the jury to agree with him. O. J. walked. As far as Darden was concerned, the trial wasn't about justice or finally even race, but about winning at any cost. According to Darden the rich defendant and his rich attorneys won. Justice lost.

When I put the book down, Jesus' words lingered: "Blessed are those who hunger and thirst for righteousness [which could as accurately have been translated *justice*], for they will be filled." Filled with what? Filled when? Filled by whom? Darden's passion for doing the right thing and getting the right results shouts from nearly every page of his book. Is there no justice? Or was Robert Frost right after all: "A jury consists of twelve persons chosen to decide who has the better lawyer."

But even then, does the better lawyer always win? And what makes the lawyer better? Winning the verdict? Fooling the jury? Polarizing the populace? Or achieving justice?

Dikaiosune (righteousness, justice) is almost always used in the New Testament for the right conduct of a person who receives the just rewards such noble behavior deserves. The judge who metes out this justice is God himself, who is pleased when people do his will. *Righteousness* has a personal and a social dimension: you can hunger and thirst to be a just, right-living person and to be declared so by God's grace; you can seek justice for all, striving to protect the rights of everyone and thus produce a just society.

Our question, in light of the Simpson trial and the multiple others like it, is this: Is genuine justice possible this side of Heaven? Peter seems to answer "yes" and "no."

> *Since everything will be destroyed in this way, what kind of people ought you to be? You ought to live holy and godly lives as you look forward to the day of God and speed its coming. That day will bring about the destruction of the heavens by fire, and the elements will melt in the heat. But in keeping with his promise we are looking forward to a new heaven and a new earth, the home of righteousness.*   2 Peter 3:11-13

Universal justice awaits the new Heaven and new earth. But in the meantime, "live holy and godly lives."

Righteousness is of God

During a famous battle between baseball's Babes, Babe Pinelli was the plate umpire and Babe Ruth the batter. Pinelli called the legendary slugger out on strikes. Ruth would have none of it. "There's forty thousand people here who know that last one was a ball, tomato head."

"Maybe so," the unflappable Pinelli retorted, "but mine is the only opinion that counts."

None of the old "what you believe is good enough for you and what I believe is good enough for me" drivel for this umpire. No way would he submit his decision to popular vote. The voice of the people was decidedly *not* the voice of God (or in this case, the umpire). Authority had spoken. The ump would not conform to the will of the crowd; they would accept his judgment. That's final.

So it is with the judgments of God, the Bible says. On those matters in which he has spoken, his word is law and his revealed will is the standard of right and wrong. Call for the vote as many times as you want, the only opinion that counts is his.

Jesus himself, who spoke as one having authority (Matthew 7:29), always acted as one under a higher authority than his own. When his cousin John hesitated to baptize him, for example, he countered, "Let it be so now; it is proper for us to do this to fulfill all righteousness" (Matthew 3:15). Obviously he felt himself under orders. For him, baptism was something God expected. No further discussion was needed.

Jesus never forgot his place. He didn't act for himself; he was God's emissary:

> *But if I do judge, my decisions are right, because I am not alone. I stand with the Father, who sent me.*   John 8:16

> *For I did not speak of my own accord, but the Father who sent me commanded me what to say and how to say it.*
>   John 12:49

> *These words you hear are not my own; they belong to the Father who sent me.*   John 14:24

Since the Father had the authority, his was the decision that mattered. Jesus was simply his agent.

In the same manner, Jesus' disciples fulfill righteousness to the extent they obey and conform to the likeness of their Lord. "Your attitude should be the same as that of Christ Jesus," Paul writes (Philippians 2:5). He sets the standard of righteousness.

Here is where, according to Jesus, the Pharisees went wrong. Scrupulously observing every jot and tittle of the Law, they managed to be superpious without being godly. So Jesus instructs his disciples, "Unless your righteousness surpasses that of the Pharisees and the teachers of the law, you will certainly not enter the kingdom of heaven" (Matthew 5:20). Better than the Pharisees? But they were the best, or at least the strictest, of their religious contemporaries. Who could be better? Jesus doesn't say so here, but he was presenting himself as the one most closely adhering to the will of the Father. What he was modeling for the disciples, they would carry on after he was gone.

*As you sent me into the world, I have sent them into the
world.*   *John 17:18*

*Again Jesus said, "Peace be with you! As the Father has sent
me, I am sending you."*   *John 20:21*

Righteousness is from God

Second Corinthians 5:21 contains one of the Bible's most
startling assertions: "God made him who had no sin to be
sin for us, so that in him we might become the righteousness of God." Jesus, the perfect one, was sacrificed for
us—not just so that we might have life, not just that we
might have our sins forgiven, and not just that we might
start living righteously and doing good things—but that
we might become the very embodiment of the righteousness of God. The Bible speaks of Jesus as the Righteous
One. Now, this verse claims, we, too are righteous ones,
not because we are so good, but because *he* is! We have
become the blessed ones of whom Psalm 32:1, 2 sings:

> *Blessed is he whose transgressions are forgiven,*
> *whose sins are covered.*
> *Blessed is the man*
> *whose sin the Lord does not count against him.*

In a real sense then, we who hunger and thirst for righteousness are eager for more of what we already have been
given, and we want to become more of what we've already
been made. We've been forgiven, so we can forgive. Our
sins have been erased, so we can treat the sins of those who
sin against us as nothing. And we who are becoming more
like Christ are eager to become even more so.

Real righteousness

What I've just written is easy to misunderstand. I must
be very clear, lest you think I'm suggesting that we somehow end up looking like the man of whom psychiatrist

Dr. Scott Peck tells. His young patient wanted nothing more than to be like Jesus, so he sported a beard and wore a robe and spent hours before the mirror practicing beatific facial expressions. His frequent meditations in public were designed not only to attract the attention of passers-by, but also in the vain hope his meditations would radiate a kind of inner peace he didn't possess. When he became impatient with Dr. Peck's treatment, he sought out a priest who was famous as a spiritual director. This priest, Peck says, deserved his fame. It took him only one session to see through the young man: "You'd sell your soul to be holy," he told him, and sent him back to the psychiatrist.[1]

The righteousness Jesus is speaking of in the Beatitude cannot be donned like a robe and sandals. Nor can it really be meditated into existence. It is in fact beyond our reach—but not beyond our grasp, if we will receive it as a free gift from God through Jesus Christ.

For the Christian, then, the focus of righteousness is not on attaining a higher degree of spiritual attainment. It is certainly not on guaranteeing personal salvation through doing all the right things. It isn't on self at all, because Christ has already taken care of our personal needs. He has made us one with himself. Baptism demonstrates our union with him. We have "clothed [ourselves] with Christ" (Galatians 3:27). Now, free from any anxiety about our relationship with him, we can turn our attention to the needs of others. Their need for justice becomes our passion.

Righteousness is doing the right thing for the right reason

Micah described it most simply, this righteousness that God expects of his people. You'll notice that the right thing is always in relation to other people.

> *He has showed you, O man, what is good.*
> *And what does the Lord require of you?*
> *To act justly and to love mercy and to walk humbly with*
> *your God.* *Micah 6:8*

Moses' charge to the Israelites does not use the word justice (righteousness), but the idea is implicit:

> *And now, O Israel, what does the Lord your God ask of you but to fear the Lord your God, to walk in all his ways, to love him, to serve the Lord your God with all your heart and with all your soul, and to observe the Lord's commands and decrees that I am giving you today for your own good?*
> *Deuteronomy 10:12, 13*

Acting justly, loving mercy, and walking humbly with God exhibit love for God. "To walk in all his ways" is the definition of righteousness. Expressing love for him also takes on specific "religious" overtones, such as in public prayers, almsgiving, and fasting (Matthew 6:1, 2-4, 5-15, 16-18). Jesus cautions against the abuse of these practices, however, because they can easily become ritualistic substitutes for the real thing. They never matter as much to Jesus as holiness, the righteousness that stems from a pure heart.

> *"Woe to you, teachers of the law and Pharisees, you hypocrites! You give a tenth of your spices—mint, dill and cummin. But you have neglected the more important matters of the law—justice, mercy and faithfulness. You should have practiced the latter, without neglecting the former."*
> *Matthew 23:23*

Scriptures urging believers to righteousness abound. Here are some examples, in the familiar King James Version translation:

> *Defend the poor and fatherless: do justice to the afflicted and needy.* *Psalm 82:3*

> *To do justice and judgment is more acceptable to the Lord*
>   *than sacrifice.*   *Proverbs 21:3*

> *Thus saith the Lord, Keep ye judgment, and do justice: for*
> *my salvation is near to come, and my righteousness to be*
> *revealed.*   *Isaiah 56:1*

In this fourth as in the earlier Beatitudes, Luke empha-
sizes the physical, as is befitting a doctor. To Matthew, the
hunger is for justice. For Luke, it's food that's wanted.

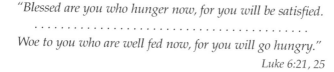

> *"Blessed are you who hunger now, for you will be satisfied.*
> . . . .
> *Woe to you who are well fed now, for you will go hungry."*
>   *Luke 6:21, 25*

Matthew and Luke's perspectives meet in Luke 14. Here
Jesus joins food and justice; his vigilance on behalf of the
poor and handicapped is the motive force behind his urging his disciples to forgo entertaining their peers who can
repay them, in favor of showing hospitality to those who
can't. They shouldn't expect any "tit for tat" in this world,
either. The real payoff comes later:

> *"When you give a luncheon or dinner, do not invite your*
> *friends, your brothers or relatives, or your rich neighbors; if you*
> *do, they may invite you back and so you will be repaid. But*
> *when you give a banquet, invite the poor, the crippled, the lame,*
> *the blind, and you will be blessed. Although they cannot repay*
> *you, you will be repaid at the resurrection of the righteous."*
>   *Luke 14:12-14*

You'll be repaid—only not now. The pursuit of righteousness is not for the impatient. This apparent inequity
gave rise to the cynical Nietzsche's famous *dictum:* "It
takes great strength to go on living, remembering that life
and injustice are synonymous." Jesus never denies that life
is painfully unjust. He believes these victims should find
someone righteous enough to right their wrongs. Jesus
wants that someone to be one of his disciples.

Righteousness satisfies

Even though many of the beatitudes, as I've already confessed, baffled me as a young Christian, this one has always made sense. A youngster can define the experience: Doing right feels good. Being rewarded for doing right is pleasurable. But even when the reward is missing, there is an intrinsic satisfaction in having lived up to the best that is in one.

That's blessing enough. Contrary to popular opinion, those who hunger and thirst for righteousness (not for superpiety or for the appearance of holiness, but for genuine righteousness) seem to live on a higher plane than others. We look up to them. We admit we're not up to their standard ourselves. They seem somehow to be more alive, more interesting, more in tune with themselves than the rest of us are. They are the saints of whom Frederick Buechner writes, "Only saints interest me as a writer. There is so much life in them. They are so in touch with, so transparent to, the mystery of things that you never know what to expect from them." He extols a saint as a life-giver, a human being "with the same sorts of hang-ups and abysses as the rest of us, but if a saint touches your life, you become alive in a new way."[2]

Elizabeth Bishop doesn't call them saints, but she's talking about the same kinds of persons, I think. "There are some people whom we envy not because they are rich or handsome or successful, although they may be all or any of these, but because everything they are or do seems to be all of a piece, so that even if they wanted to they could not be or do otherwise."[3]

Do these descriptions explain, at least in part, the fascination Jesus held for his friend Mary? For her, Jesus had "so much life" in him, was "so in touch with, so transparent to, the mystery of things," his touch made you "come alive in a new way"; he was so "all of a piece" he "could not be or do otherwise." Absorbing his soul-expanding words, she sat at his feet oblivious to everything else. Her sister's remonstrances couldn't move her. She was transfixed (see Luke 10:38-42; John 12:1-8).

The kitchen beckoned Martha, and she obeyed. Mary could not be bothered by the merely *urgent;* Jesus was introducing her to the truly *important.* She wanted more. He was, from Buechner's perspective, the ultimate saint. She hungered to know Jesus better, to hear him more clearly, to be drawn into the kingdom where he was more present even than in her home. She had glimpsed eternal reality. The kitchen could wait.

Earlier I told you about my horseback riding in Washington. You weren't the first to hear the story. When Joy and I returned from our all-family vacation in the Pacific Northwest, I wanted to tell everyone about everything we did that week, including the horseback riding but, aware of how boring other people's vacation stories can be, I manfully restrained myself.

Until I saw Bernie. We met on our way into the church building one Sunday morning. I could tell Bernie. This longtime pal is almost as old as I am, and even more ready to take on challenges perhaps better befitting young men. With his ever-present can of Dr. Pepper in hand, my crew-cutted friend looks like a man more at home buried beneath some automobile hood (he's a mechanic) or at the end of a water-ski rope or on his motorcycle than at a prayer meeting. You'd be surprised to learn he's a church leader, I suspect. My kind of guy. As we headed into the building, I hurriedly described our rides on the Smiths' magnificent Arabians, and narrated our white-water rafting escapades on Oregon's Deschutes River and the jet skiing on the Willamette. I knew he'd share my excitement. He said something pretty forgettable, but then, with glistening eyes, he broke into his broadest grin to tell me, "I just read Revelation. Awesome. I read it from start to finish. It makes sense when you do it that way." His enthusiasm shamed me. I was the preacher, after all, the one who should be sharing my latest scriptural discoveries with him. But I was terribly proud to be his pastor. I wanted to discuss my recreation; he wanted to talk about God's Word. His zest for learning scriptural truth hasn't waned, either. Bernie's reading through the Bible now. He started with—and has completed—the New Testament and is on his way through the Old Testament. (I hope he can maintain his ardor as he trudges through Leviticus and Numbers.)

For the moment we were playing our version of Mary and Martha. He was discovering more of God, soaking up the new truth he'd found, hungry for more. I was distracted about many things.

It won't surprise you, in light of our discussion in this chapter, that Bernie is working harder than ever as a sponsor of our church's college ministry. Without a college education himself, he's committed to reaching as many young people for Christ as possible. He and his wife, Judy, open their home for meetings, parties, even for free room and board. Several of the church's college-age interns have moved in with them for varying lengths of time. When a mission project is announced, they are the first to volunteer.

Very few people would call Bernie and Judy "righteous." If you used the word on them, they'd laugh or blush, or both. Yet their hunger for righteousness is voracious—and gets stronger with the passing years. They remind me of C. S. Lewis's observation, "I don't agree that if anyone were completely a new creature, you and I would necessarily recognize him as such. It takes holiness to detect holiness."[4]

No, the righteous don't all look alike. Lewis is right: They're not always easy to recognize. What's pretty obvious, though, is the hunger.

It will be satisfied. They'll see to it. So will God.

[1]M. Scott Peck, M.D., *A World Waiting to be Born.* New York, et al: Bantam Books, 1993, p. 256.

[2]*Christianity Today,* September 4, 1992, p. 44.

[3]Quoted in *Context,* December 1, 1994, p. 5.

[4]C. S. Lewis, "Letter to Stuart Robertson (6 May 1962)," *The Business of Heaven,* ed. Walter Hooper. Great Britain: Collins Fount Paperbacks, 1984, p. 216.

6

Heavenly Mercy!

Blessed are the merciful,
for they will be shown mercy.
Matthew 5:7

In the last chapter, justice (a synonym of righteousness) was our subject. Justice is getting what's coming to you. Now we turn our attention to mercy, which is getting better than what's coming to you, better than you deserve.

In a well-worn story that remains a favorite, the notorious nineteenth-century Mexican bank robber, Jorge Rodriguez, has made another of his bank-robbing forays into Texas. This time a Texas Ranger spots him. Trailing him to the targeted bank, the Ranger witnesses the robbery and then follows Rodriguez back across the border to a cantina where the hustler is relaxing with a drink. The Ranger draws his .45 and takes his bead. "I know who you are, Rodriguez. I know what you've been doing, and unless you give back all of the money you've taken from those banks, I'm going to blow your brains out."

The thief doesn't understand English, but it's no problem. Before the thief can say, "No comprendo," a timid-looking Mexican speaks up. "I know both languages. I'll translate for you." With that he turns and begins to translate.

Rodriguez knows he's been caught fair and square. "Tell the Ranger I want to live, that I haven't spent a single cent of that money. If he will go to the town well, face north, and count down seven stones, there will be a loose one. Pull it out and behind it he will find all the money I've taken."

The little Mexican turns back to the Ranger and translates, "Jorge Rodriguez is a brave man. He says he is ready to die."

Where greed is, there mercy is not.

My mother was always the proper lady. Her children never heard her swear. Her strongest expletive was, "Merciful heavens!" She was never known to utter a single "Merciful earth!" Neither has anyone else used it, as far as I can tell. It wouldn't be your most satisfying oath, would it? For mercy, you look upward, from whence comes your help. You don't look earthward. Earthlings aren't big on mercy.

If it is true, as we concluded in the last chapter, that saints (the just, the righteous) live on a plane above the rest of us, then the merciful are on the highest level of all. They not only work for a just society, but they labor to make life better for others, even before they deserve it.

Charles Colson writes of a young woman named Christy who belongs to a group of "saints" who regularly visit terminally ill AIDS patients in a Washington, DC hospital. This was in the early 1980s, when America was in a panic over the disease. Victims were isolated; even medical personnel were afraid of physical contact with them. Because the patients usually had moved away from their families, they had no visitors. None, that is, except Christy and her friends, who cheered them with their smiles—and postage stamps, stationery, books, tapes, and cookies. They quietly shared their faith and had the joy of seeing several of the patients accept Christ as Savior. In a prayer memo Christy wrote, "They are socially unacceptable because of their lifestyle and medically unacceptable because of their diseases. They are scared. They are dying. They are unsaved." As far as Christy was concerned, these were reasons enough for the ministry. Was she afraid? "No, we believe we are doing the will of God."[1]

In the early 1980s, hers was a pretty heroic attitude. You may remember that at the same time many preachers were thundering in their pulpits that AIDS was God's justice on homosexuals. They were getting what they deserved. Christy and her friends were giving them better, in the spirit of the apostle Paul, who wrote, "Christ died for the ungodly. . . . God demonstrates his own love for us in this: While we were still sinners, Christ died for us" (Romans 5:6, 8).

One of my heroes is a man whom Jesus also admired. Although this person lived only in a good story (The Parable of the Good Samaritan), he is as well celebrated a personality in Western civilization as any historical figure you can name. He's the man we'd all like to have around when we're in trouble. He's given his "name" to merciful benefactors everywhere.

Margaret Thatcher discounts his reputation a little. She insists no one would remember the good Samaritan if he'd had only good intentions; he had money, too. She's too cynical. Lots of people have the money; what they don't have is the character. The Samaritan practiced the love Christians talks about, but fall short of practicing. We've traveled the lonely roads and seen the victims of life's brutality—and like the priest and Levite, we've crossed over to the other side, rationalizing that we are in a hurry and it would be dangerous to stop and probably the man got what he had coming to him anyway and . . . and . . . and.

The world's most famous modern-day good Samaritan is Mother Teresa. Tales of her missions of mercy are recounted worldwide. Most of them are true. Some, like the following one, are probably apocryphal. I first heard it many years ago, attributed to someone else. In this version Mother Teresa is dressing the wounds of a dying leper. An American tourist watches her for a while, then asks her permission to take a picture. When he draws close enough to frame the scene, the tourist is repulsed by the blood, the smell, and the leper's disfigurement. "Sister," he confesses, "I wouldn't do what you are doing for ten million dollars!"

"Neither would I my friend, neither would I." From everything we know of the sister, if it didn't happen exactly as the story tells it, it could have.

This one did happen. Another American was visiting Mother Teresa and, inspired, yet uneasy, in the presence of such loving care of society's most unfortunate, he confessed, "I'm typical of many Americans who want to stop hunger and pain but who feel overwhelmed by the bigness of the problems." She pointed her finger and spoke intensely. "Tell your American friends they don't have to go around the world to find people who suffer. In America there are many needs. People are lonely. They feel alienated. . . . Some people are so lonely they want to die. They need love . . . especially the old people. If we have Jesus' love, we must share it."[2]

Her point is scriptural. Mercy leads to ministry, as in the case of the apostle Paul, who locates the motivation for his life's work in God's mercy: "Therefore, since through God's mercy we have this ministry, we do not lose heart" (2 Corinthians 4:1). What motivates Paul moves most

Christian ministers, doesn't it? From *God's* mercy have come our ministries. From our ministries, others will receive mercy.

What, then, does this mercy look like?

Mercy looks like empathy

Why, when others stepped around the victim on the road to Jericho, did the Samaritan come to the rescue? Surely he, too, had pressing appointments. No doubt he could tell that the victim was a Jew—and Jews and Samaritans had no truck with each other. The racial animosity between them was deep and bitter. Don't you imagine he was as reluctant to become involved as anyone else?

So why did he do it? My guess is that his benevolence grew out of personal experience. He had been a victim himself. He'd been there, so he understood. Jesus had been warned about Samaritans all his life; they were a despised race. As an alien among foreigners, the Samaritan was no stranger to mental and perhaps even physical abuse. He may even have been rescued in the past by some merciful soul, perhaps—one would like to think—by a sympathetic Jew. His empathy moved him to action.

Sometimes, even if you can't *do* anything to help, empathy is enough by itself. A little girl was pretty late getting home from school. When she arrived, her worried mother wanted to know why she was so late.

"I had to help another girl. She was in trouble."

"What did you do to help her?"

"Oh, I sat down and helped her cry."

Her mother would understand. Your writer, a typical male, would have asked a thousand questions. "What was wrong with her? What was the problem? Should we go back and do something for her?" Tears alone would have exasperated me. What good would they do? But, having lived a few years as a husband and father, I've been taught better. Sometimes an empathetic heart—

expressed in a good shared cry—is all that's needed.

It's virtually impossible to discuss this subject without mentioning another of my heroes, Abraham Lincoln. Accounts of the Civil War President's compassion are still retold, often in wonderment that a politician could have had such a servant's heart. Not long ago I ran across an instance of his mercy that I hadn't read before. In 1863, midway through the war, Lincoln was on an excursion aboard the steamer *Hartford*. He spotted a narrow, iron-bound door he hadn't seen before. Asking about it, he was told it was a "sweatbox," a three-foot by three-foot, poorly ventilated cubicle. Its stifling steam heat could quickly tame a rebellious sailor. Thousands of American seamen were subjected to the treatment every year.

The President decided to learn more about it for himself. Doffing his hat, he gave orders to open at a signal from him. Then he folded his six-foot-plus frame into its constricting walls. The door was shut behind him. Steam quickly poured in. It didn't take him long to get the effect. After just three minutes he gave the signal.

Emerging from his enforced steam bath, Lincoln ordered Secretary Welles that in the future the sweatbox should never be allowed on any American ship. Within a few years, Great Britain , France, Germany and other European countries followed suit.[3]

The President's experience led to new empathy for suffering seamen. His empathy led him to take action. That's the order of mercy.

Mercy does simple, little things

The merciful don't go in for the grand statement; they don't major in spectaculars nor play to the galleries. They do what they can with what they have, to make a positive difference to someone. Whether they are noticed or not doesn't concern them.

At a Food for the Hungry seminar a couple of years ago,

a man in the audience asked the presenter, a veteran of many years of famine relief work, "How do you handle compassion fatigue?" I was eager to hear the answer, because our church is bombarded with requests from people dropping in for a handout and from agencies of every kind writing for dollars to get them through their latest emergency. After awhile, you turn a deaf ear. You can't bear to hear yet another plea. The seminar leader responded quietly, "You simply do what you can." Then he quoted Larry Ward, Food for the Hungry's founder. "It comes down to one life," Ward would tell his coworkers. "People die one at a time. We can help them one at a time."

We were given an excellent example of the principle. A Hunger Corps engineer was assigned to a village ten kilometers from the nearest water. Think of the daily labor of the women who had to carry that water to their homes. The greatest blessing of their lives would be something we take for granted in our country. The water comes to us. To make the village women's lives simpler, the engineer constructed a basic aqueduct to conduct the water from its source to the village. One trained man, one act of mercy, transformed the village. (By the way, during his second three-year term he applied what he learned in this village and helped eight hundred more villages, helping a hundred thousand people. What began as a simple task for this skilled man became a life-giving mission benefiting thousands.)

I have admired Food for the Hungry's development projects. They do the elementary but necessary things that lift people's standard of living. This engineer exemplifies the agency's policy. He didn't go for a Grand Coulee Dam, or import technological marvels beyond the people's ability to maintain, or attempt to "Westernize" the villages. He gave them water by means of an aqueduct they could maintain after he left them.

Mercy may lie in something you don't do, for example

in a picture you don't take or a story you don't tell. Sometimes I become so disgusted with today's intrusive news media I swear to renounce television news forever. Their abusive snooping into people's private lives often inflicts intolerable pain. Older Americans can reflect nostalgically on a kinder era, when Franklin D. Roosevelt was our president. Crippled by polio, this man whom most historians rank among our half dozen greatest presidents, could not be elected today. The media would see to it. But when he was in office in the 1930s and 1940s, Roosevelt was never humiliated by a press determined to broadcast pictures of the president laboriously pulling himself to his feet. His muscles atrophied by polio, FDR couldn't walk or stand without assistance, yet most Americans were not aware of the extent of his disability. Newsmen turned the other way when he fell. As far as most of the nation was concerned, he was a vigorous, healthy leader. Today, claiming "the public has a right to know," journalists and photographers would show him no mercy.

It's a simple thing, this permitting a politician to retain his dignity. But it's merciful.

Mercy is always something beautiful

In a crude world, mercy moves with grace. "When she touches a thing," Henry James writes of Mme. De Vionnet in *The Ambassadors,* "the ugliness, God knows how, goes out of it." The careful Samaritan, gently attending ugly wounds, lifting a broken man onto his donkey, arranging for his stay in the inn, not haggling over the price of the room, taking on himself any additional expenses—his every merciful act is a thing of beauty.

If the Samaritan's tenderness weren't so rare, there wouldn't be a story here. But mercy is beautiful in large measure because it is so uncommon. It's like carnations in Bangkok.

As our bus inched its way through the city's crowded

marketplace, we were surprised at the proliferation of orchids. They seemed to be as common as, say, carnations are in the States. What American male of my generation doesn't remember the first time he bought his sweetheart an orchid? The costly gift was a sure winner. But in Thailand, our guide informed us, to give a girl an orchid would be to insult her. A common orchid? How gauche! What would really woo the girl would be something rarer, more expensive. Something like—yes, like a carnation!

"Blessed are the merciful," our Lord says. He wouldn't bother to commend them if they were commonplace. Mercy is just not something we expect from one another. We've hardened ourselves; we have to look out for Number One, because we've convinced ourselves no one else will. When someone does us a small favor, we hardly know how to act. We are like a lady sitting in a wheelchair at the airport gate. The attentive flight attendant assured her she would be taken to the plane ahead of the rest of the passengers and assisted into her seat. Then, when the plane landed, she would be met by another attendant with a wheelchair. She didn't have to worry about a thing. She would be taken care of.

"How nice of you to care for me without my having to pay extra," the lady thanked her.

Mercy is not self-conscious

Mercy's beauty consists, at least in part, in its modesty. It doesn't announce its virtue "with trumpets, as the hypocrites do in the synagogues and on the streets, to be honored by men" (Matthew 6:2). It possesses a simplicity, a matter-of-factness, an almost to-be-taken-for-granted quality. Merciful persons are just *naturally* concerned about others. They resemble the villager of whom Philip Hallie writes. Seeing a man putting a very large bill into a box for earthquake or flood victims on other side of the planet, Hallie asked him who the victims were. "He looked at me in surprise and said, 'Oh, I don't know. They're people.'"[4] They're people, and they're victims, and I have the means to help. That's reason enough for a sacrificial offering. Isn't it?

He was just doing what comes naturally. But is it natural? Anthropologist Richard Leakey thinks so. Disagreeing with most subscribers to the theory of evolution, Leakey does not believe primitive human beings separated themselves from chimps and baboons by their superior intelligence. What distinguished them from the rest of the animal kingdom, he hypothesizes, was their sharing. Their looking out for one another made community possible and enabled them to rise above the beasts. According to Leakey's reasoning, sharing is not only a virtue but is humanity's primary defining characteristic. Failure to share is failing to be human. When viewed from the outside, especially when the stronger takes care of the weaker, sharing looks like mercy. Leakey starts far from the Bible in his quest to understand human nature, but he arrives at the same place.

According to this interpretation, then, the good Samaritan is the *human* being in Jesus' parable. I don't know what Leakey would call the priest and the Levite.

Mercy just does what God did

As far as Jesus is concerned, the priest and Levite represent formal religion, but the Samaritan represents God. Jesus is answering the query, "Who is my neighbor?" What makes his story unforgettable, though, is his portrait of this unexpectedly gracious Samaritan who is so, well, so much like God. The Bible is replete with references to God's mercy, for he is a "gracious and merciful God" (Nehemiah 9:31; see also Psalm 25:6; Daniel 9:18; and 1 Peter 1:3). King David, no stranger to human violence, confided to his prophet Gad, "I am in deep distress. Let me fall into the hands of the Lord, for his mercy is very great; but do not let me fall into the hands of men" (1 Chronicles 21:13). Men would attack him, he knew, but God would protect even as he protects us: "Cast all your anxiety on him because he cares for you" (1 Peter 5:7). He is, after all the one of whom John writes, "For God so loved the world that he gave his one and only Son, that whoever believes in him shall not perish but have eternal life" (John 3:16). What greater example of mercy has there ever been?

In this, as in God's other virtues, we are to imitate him.

> *"For I desire mercy, not sacrifice, and acknowledgment of God rather than burnt offerings."* Hosea 6:6; Matthew 9:13

> *"He has showed you, O man, what is good. And what does the Lord require of you? To act justly and to love mercy and to walk humbly with your God."* Micah 6:8

> *"This is what the Lord Almighty says: 'Administer true justice; show mercy and compassion to one another.'"*
>
> Zechariah 7:9

Mercy simply imitates God, whose mercy "is very great."

You can count on it. You can count on him.

Can he count on us?

---

[1]Charles Colson, *Who Speaks for God?* Westchester, Ill: Crossway Books, 1985, p. 22.

[2]Ruth Jutila Chamberlin, "Meeting Mother Teresa," *World Vision,* March 1981, p. 5.

[3]Emanuel Hertz Scrapbooks, in B. A. Botkin, *A Civil War Treasury of Tales, Legends and Folklore.* New York: Promontory Press, 1967, pp. 242, 243.

[4]Philip Hallie, *Lest Innocent Blood Be Shed.* New York et al: Harper Torchbooks, Harper and Row, 1979, p. 285.

7

The Best Kind of Absentmindedness

Blessed are the pure in heart,
for they will see God.
Matthew 5:8

"Teacher, what good thing must I do to get eternal life?"
If ever there was anyone who could convince you he sin-
cerely wants to please God, this petitioner in Matthew 19
is the man. He impresses Jesus. Mark's narrative of this
encounter says Jesus "loved him" (Mark 10:21). No wonder. By his own account, he seems to be "hungering and
thirsting for righteousness." He has kept all the command-
ments. Here he is earnestly checking with Jesus to see
whether he has left anything out of his spiritual disciplines. He is the kind of man every mother dreams of for
her daughter: Upright, religious, successful. And rich.

There is just one thing wrong. He isn't pure.

Oh, don't misunderstand. He isn't sexually immoral. (It says a lot about us, doesn't it, that when we call another person *impure*, the word immediately takes on sexual overtones?) That kind of impurity isn't this man's problem. In fact, this may be the first time anyone has ever suggested he lacks anything. He seems to have it all. All except one thing, as Jesus immediately discerns. He prescribes the only cure: "If you want to be perfect, go, sell your possessions and give to the poor, and you will have treasure in heaven. Then come, follow me" (Matthew 19:21).

It sounds as if Jesus is attacking the man's wealth, but look closer. What is at stake is the man's integrity. He doesn't mean what he says, or at the very least he is being less than honest. He is asking about eternal life, but if that were truly his goal, he wouldn't be disappointed. What he wants is within his grasp, but he can't take hold of it until he releases his death-grip on his possessions. Jesus zeroes in on his holdings because it is in them, rather than in God, that he trusts. Jesus offers him a fair exchange. Give up what you can't keep anyway for what you can't lose. A more than fair exchange.

He won't make the trade. Instead, he walks away, "because he had great wealth" (or, as we preachers love to add, "because his great wealth had him"). He has a divided, not a pure, heart.

John Woolman has long been acknowledged by students of American literature and religious history as a remarkable example of purity of heart. He's not widely remembered now, but he has inspired generations of his countrymen. His journals expose the sheer goodness of the man. Woolman's fame didn't come to him through political or economic influence, but through his spiritual purity. One fan, Harry Emerson Fosdick, writes that John Woolman lived the Beatitudes, being "poor in spirit, meek, a

mourner, pure in heart, a peacemaker, ready to be persecuted for righteousness' sake, and he hungered and
thirsted with a passion for what was eternally right and
good." What most impressed Fosdick, though, "was his
gentleness, his tenderness, his absolute simplicity. *The
divided will, which is so much in evidence even in most good
persons, did not appear in him.* There was no duplicity, no
doubleness, no utilitarian aims; self-seeking was as completely washed out of his heart as it can possibly be
washed out and have any life of personality left. Perhaps
the most striking passage in the *Journal* is the one in which
he heard a divine voice say, 'John Woolman is dead,' and
discovered that it meant, 'I [John Woolman] am crucified
with Christ: nevertheless I live; yet not I, but Christ liveth
in me'" (Galatians 2:20).[1]

Woolman's singleness of mind is what Jesus means by a
"pure heart." It is, as Kierkegaard has defined it, "to will
one thing." It is at the opposite pole of the rich young
man's contradictory quest, vying for eternal life with the
one hand while hanging on for dear life to his possessions
with the other.

Frederick Buechner would not have me be so hard on
this man. The contemporary Christian novelist doubts that
any of us answers Jesus' call with anything other than
"our own unending ambiguous motives."

> The voice that we hear over our shoulders never
> says, "First be sure that your motives are pure and self-
> less and then follow me." If it did, then we could none
> of us follow. So when later the voice says, "Take up
> your cross and follow me," at least part of what is
> meant by 'cross' is our realization that we are seldom
> any less than nine parts fake.[2]

To admit mixed motives is one thing, however, and to
claim they're unconquerable is another. Buechner correctly
points out the simplicity of Jesus' call: Follow me. Or, in

the case of this rich young man, "Give away your possessions and follow me." Clear-cut, simple instructions.
Purity of heart consists of *doing* what is required, regardless of warring emotions or conflicting motives.

In praising the pure in heart, Jesus echoes earlier Scriptures.

> *Who may ascend the hill of the Lord?*
> . . . .
> *He who has clean hands and a pure heart,*
> *who does not lift up his soul to an idol*
> *or swear by what is false.*   *Psalm 24:3, 4*

> *Create in me a pure heart, O God,*
> *and renew a steadfast spirit within me.*   *Psalm 51:10*

> *The Lord detests the thoughts of the wicked,*
> *but those of the pure are pleasing to him.*
>   *Proverbs 15:26*

Later, the apostle Paul repeats the same concern:

> *I am jealous for you with a godly jealousy. I promised you to*
> *one husband, to Christ, so that I might present you as a pure*
> *virgin to him.*   *2 Corinthians 11:2*

His warning is vivid:

> *But I am afraid that just as Eve was deceived by the serpent's*
> *cunning, your minds may somehow be led astray from your*
> *sincere and pure devotion to Christ.*   *2 Corinthians 11:3*

Attention wanders. To will one thing, to be devoted
with single-mindedness, to resist temptation, to cling to
Christ when other suitors tease—such are the disciplines
of the pure in heart.

Purity of heart: Sanctified absentmindedness

G. K. Chesterton's forgetfulness was legendary. His
friends teased and his critics scolded for his missed
appointments. He was infamous for taking wrong trains

and then calling his wife to tell her where he was and ask where he should have been. Their jibes about his absent-mindedness, good-natured and otherwise, didn't offend him. Instead, he offered the best defense I've seen on the subject: "I am not absentminded," he protested. "It is the presence of mind that makes me unaware of everything else."

Exactly. The more the mind and heart are concentrating on the object at hand, the more oblivious they are to outside interference. The scientist forgets his supper in the drama of his laboratory. Children in the sandbox honestly can't hear mother calling them in at nap time. The saint at prayer is oblivious to the passing hours. The businessman beset with personnel problems actually doesn't see the other passengers on the train. This is the quality that Chesterton calls "present-mindedness"; it is the kind of "sanctified absentmindedness" Jesus has in mind when he speaks of a pure heart. "One thing I do," said the apostle Paul of his own present-mindedness: "Forgetting what is behind and straining toward what is ahead, I press on toward the goal to win the prize for which God has called me heavenward in Christ Jesus" (Philippians 3:13, 14). Everything else is irrelevant. He is not present to distractions.

Paul is like the sculptor answering his visitor's question about his technique. How would he sculpt a horse out of the block of marble on his studio floor? "I will take a hammer and a chisel and knock off everything that doesn't look like a horse," he explains. The pure in heart simply remove from their lives whatever doesn't look like Christ.

I know, I know—*simply* was the wrong word. This advice is much more easily given than followed. Many committed Christians yearn to live before God in such simplicity, knowing nothing but God, desiring nothing but to please him, worshiping him, like the elders in the book of Revelation, without ceasing. But there are bills to pay

and laundry to wash and babies to change and a boss to
satisfy and a hectic life to live. All kinds of things in our
lives don't look like the Christ we want to sculpt in us—
and they will not be chiseled away.

Sanctified absentmindedness requires discipline; perhaps even more, it requires retraining. The mind must be
taught what the heart senses, that there is much more to
life than tending to trivial duties, more than bringing
home Olympic gold. This retraining is what Paul is seeking in Philippians 4:8:

> *Finally, brothers, whatever is true, whatever is noble, what-
> ever is right, whatever is pure, whatever is lovely, whatever is
> admirable—if anything is excellent or praiseworthy—think
> about such things.*

Purity of heart:
Seeking the best advice you can get

If our goal is to think about true, noble, right, pure,
lovely, admirable things, where do we find them? "How
can a young man keep his way pure?" asks the psalmist.
"By living according to your word," he answers (Psalm
119:9). His is a timely answer. Elsewhere he says, "I have
hidden your word in my heart that I might not sin against
you" (Psalm 119:11). You can be casually religious without
filling yourself with a knowledge of God's Word, but you
can't be pure in heart. To strive for sinlessness is to desire
to be taught when ignorant, guided when straying, disciplined when wrong, and goaded when lazy.

Purity of heart and casual religiosity just can't co-exist.
Christopher Lasche believes the laid-back nature of what
he calls "the New Age replacements for religion" is exactly
what's wrong with them. "They soothe the conscience
instead of rubbing it the wrong way." By contrast, he
insists, New Testament spirituality is "not a search for religious experience nor a self-help movement, nor a philoso-

phy, nor a search for enlightenment, nor an idea or a technique of meditation, but simply a life lived in Christ."[3]

Lasche's reminder is instructive. Spirituality is often equated with a regimen of prayer and Bible study, a moral improvement program, a denominationally approved set of rules, or even personal ethical advancement. These are variations of the form of mistake some of Jesus' contemporaries, the Pharisees, were wont to make. In their otherwise admirable search for spiritual excellence they often came across as quite "holier than thou." Their sense of superiority earned more than one rebuke from Jesus.

And a backhanded one from C. S. Lewis, who decided that while both cats and dogs have consciences, "the dog, being an honest, humble person, always has a bad one, but the cat . . . always has a good one. When he sits and stares you out of countenance he is thanking God that he is not as these dogs, or these humans, or even as these other cats!"[4] Lewis must have met the same cats I've known, supremely contented with their magnificence, quite unwilling to change their ways. They are the ruling class, bringing an entire household of humans into submission. They need no guides, they acknowledge no masters. They have arrived.

But the dogs of my acquaintance have been teachable, devoted, master-pleasing lovers. Some of them have seemed, well, pure in heart, like those of whom Jesus said, "Blessed . . . are those who hear the word of God and obey it" (Luke 11:28).

Purity of heart: Head and heart conjoined

And this is my prayer: that your love may abound more and more in knowledge and depth of insight, so that you may be able to discern what is best and may be pure and blameless until the day of Christ, filled with the fruit of righteousness that comes through Jesus Christ—to the glory and praise of God.

Philippians 1:9-11

Look closely at what Paul puts together in this brief
paragraph:
- love
- knowledge and depth of insight
- discernment of the best
- purity and blamelessness
- the fruit of righteousness
    (that comes through Jesus Christ)
- the glory and praise of God

This list reminds us of another cluster of characteristics
that together constitute the fruit of the spirit: Love, joy,
peace, patience, kindness, gentleness, faithfulness, and
self-control. Each characteristic depends on all the others
to come to fruition.

Just so, love grows in knowledge and depth of insight,
which of course grow best in the soil of love. Discernment
requires a deep look, and wise knowing, a loving compre-
hension. Purity and blamelessness are both the product
and the source of righteousness.

And everything is to the praise and glory of God.

The pure in heart, then, are of a piece, an integrated
whole that runs deep. What they seem to be on the outside they are all the way to the core of their being.
Hypocrisy is foreign to their nature, as Harvard psycholo-
gist Gordon Allport discovered in his study of the nature
of religious behavior in relation to bigotry and prejudice.
He found that a majority of adherents in religion—in any
religion—could be described as *extrinsically* religious, that
is, religious on the outside. They are the *users* of religion.
Going to church, for example, can be a relatively easy way
to gain status in the eyes of the community, to win friends
and make good business contacts, to become more self-
confident and even more influential. So they go to church.
The extrinsically religious often use their belief to defend
themselves against unpleasant reality. Perhaps the most

useful aspect of this "outside" religion, however, is its self-sanctioning quality. Such believers assure themselves that God sees things exactly the way they do; they are right-eous as God is righteous, because God is like them. According to Allport, the extrinsically religious person *turns to God but does not turn away from self.* Like the rich young man whom we met at the beginning of the chapter, they talk about Heaven but live very much in this world. Their religion serves *them;* it gives them a sense of security, status, and self-esteem.

As you would expect, Allport's tests proved these "religious on the outside" people exhibit strong tendencies toward prejudice and bigotry. Their number is legion. They can perhaps best be characterized as Metternich described Tsar Alexander I of Russia (1801-1825): "Moving from one form of worship to another, from one religion to another, he stirred up everything, built nothing: everything about him was on the surface."[5]

On the other hand, Allport found some people who were what he called *intrinsically* religious, "religious on the inside." They love their Lord with heart and soul and mind. Admittedly, this is a smaller number of people. Allport reported these believers had "a deeply interiorized religious faith and were totally committed to it. Their love of God was integral and all-encompassing. It was an open faith, with room for scientific and emotional facts. Intrinsic religious love was a hunger for and commitment to oneness with God and all others. The intrinsically religious had little prejudice or bigotry. They practiced what they preached and evidenced a striking humility."[6] The toughness of their minds meets the compassion of their hearts in the pursuit of God's will. They are pure in heart.

In Mark 7:14-23, Jesus speaks directly to the "extrinsically" religious. He boldly denounces the many rituals of purification imposed on his countrymen (originally there were three, for sexual discharges, leprosy, contact with a dead body), and calls for purity of heart. It isn't what a man eats or drinks that defiles him, Jesus insists, but what comes out of him. And what Jesus says comes out gives a pretty clear picture of the opposite of spiritual purity: "For from within, out of men's hearts, come evil thoughts, sexual immorality, theft, murder, adultery, greed, malice, deceit, lewdness, envy, slander, arrogance and folly. All these evils come from inside and make a man 'unclean.'"

Purity of heart: the goal, the means

Several years ago I read Philip Hallie's *Lest Innocent Blood Be Shed*[7] a moving account of how a small French village became a place of refuge for Jews fleeing the murderous Nazis. As Pastor Trocme went about organizing the effort, he first convinced his presbyterial council in the winter of 1941 to establish a village residence that would be funded by the Quakers. Then he recruited his second cousin, Daniel Trocme, to take over that residence. He thought of his cousin as "an intellectual given to rather vague ideas, and often rather absentminded, but totally free of selfishness, and possessed of a conscience without gaps." He was, in other words, pure in heart, possessing what I earlier called sanctified absentmindedness and a tough heart-mind love.

"A conscience without gaps." Can you think of a better way to describe purity of heart? Does it feel like what the little boy tried to describe to his mother? "I've got something inside me I can't do what I want to with!"

That's a start, but only a start. When the tug-of-war between will and conscience ends with the will's submission, purity has been achieved. Old temptations lose their allure. The pure in heart "flee the evil desires of youth, and pursue righteousness, faith, love and peace" (2 Timothy 2:22). They do this because they have now "put on Christ," ("clothed" themselves in Christ) in both senses of the word. They don't have any interest in anything now but becoming more and more like Jesus, so they "put on" Christ the way a Roman legionary would dress for battle, with his helmet, breastplate, shield, and sword (see Ephesians 6:10-17), or, to borrow from the Greek theater, they "put on" Christ the way an actor dons the character he is portraying. He "becomes" his stage character.

Like the soldier, and especially like the actor, our goal is to become *like* Christ; the means is to put *on* Christ.

"Blessed are the pure in heart, for they will see God." It's an old axiom and true: You see what you are looking for. More than anything or anyone else in their lives, the pure in heart are looking for God. They will succeed.

[1]Harry Emerson Fosdick, *Rufus Jones Speaks to Our Time.* New York: The Macmillan Company, 1951, p. 208. Italics mine.

[2]From *The Magnificent Defeat.* Quoted in Keith Miller, *Habitation of Dragons,* p. 97.

[3]Lasche's New Oxford Review (April 1991) is quoted in "Blinded by the 'Lite,'" *Christianity Today* editorial, September 12, 1994, p. 14.

[4]From *Letters to an American Lady,* 21 March 1955, p. 40; quoted in *The Quotable Lewis,* ed. Wayne Martindale and Jerry Root. Wheaton: Tyndale House Publishers, 1989, p. 118.

[5]Paul Johnson, *The Birth of the Modern.* New York: Harper Collins, 1988, pp. 94, 95.

[6]John Bradshaw, *Creating Love.* New York, et al: Bantam Books, 1992, pp. 226, 227.

[7]New York, et al: Harper Torchbooks, 1979, p. 206.

8

The Children of God

Blessed are the peacemakers,
for they will be called sons of God.
Matthew 5:9

If Esther Augsberger has had her way by now, there is a
new symbol for this Beatitude in Washington, DC It's a
giant, a sixteen-foot plow near the District's historic court-
house, close to both the main police building and the
mayor's residence.

Appearances deceive. Esther Augsberger exudes the
gentle graciousness of a kindly, petite grandmother. On
first meeting her, you would not guess her profession—at
least I didn't. We met at a meeting of the Coalition of
Christian Colleges and Universities. Her husband, Myron,
was conducting his final annual meeting as president of
the Washington-based organization. When she was for-

mally introduced at the banquet, her work as a sculptor
was highlighted, but what really piqued my curiosity was
when we learned her chief tool is a blowtorch. I couldn't
picture so refined a woman as a welder.

This artist/welder is a lady on a mission. Drawing
inspiration from Micah 4:3 and Isaiah 2:4, she has been
"beating swords [guns in this case] into plowshares." The
mission came to her in 1994 while the Augsbergers were
viewing the television news. The city police announced a
two-week amnesty program. Boots and gift certificates
were to be handed out in exchange for weapons. The
guns-for-goods swap would net the department more
than six thousand guns during the two-week period.
Esther asked for half the guns for the project that was
forming in her mind. The request was granted.

Three thousand guns welded into a sixteen-foot plow.
Instruments of violence were transformed into a symbol of
peace. This was her dream. The Augsbergers are Mennon-
ites. Pacifists. Esther's sculpture would represent their
hope that the city might take a stand against violence,
against the all-too-routine killing of Washington's inner-
city youth. As many people are killed yearly in the District
as in war-ravaged Israeli-occupied territories.

You'd think everyone would applaud this peaceful conversion of tools of destruction to a symbol of peace. To the
contrary. Angry gun-lovers have stormed her workshop to
protest this waste of perfectly good weapons!

Far from intimidated, Esther carried on with her work.
She also sought volunteers to make models for every high
school in the District of Columbia, since most Washington
students have never seen a plow. She hoped these models
would inspire young people and gang leaders to lay down
their guns.

It may be a naive dream. Peacemakers usually seem
innocent to cynics. I admire Esther for her contribution to
the quest for peace. Doubters may scoff, but as I learned

more of her amazing scheme, I had to ask myself, "And you, Lawson, what's your plan? What design for world peace do you have to offer? And if world peace seems too ambitious for you, what's your proposal for neighborhood peace? And what are you *doing* about it?"

Unfortunately, Mrs. Augsberger's plowshare is not the only symbol that comes to mind while reading the seventh Beatitude. There is one far more disturbing. A few years ago the Pentagon proudly announced its newest missile, "The Peacemaker." It has the capability of wiping out vast numbers of the enemy. Here's the Defense Department's design for establishing peace: Annihilate your enemies.

You can't help thinking of Jeremiah, can you?

> From the least to the greatest, all are greedy for gain; prophets and priests alike, all practice deceit. They dress the wound of my people as though it were not serious. "Peace, peace," they say, when there is no peace.   Jeremiah 6:13, 14

Anyway, there you have them, two symbols of peace-making: Esther Augsberger's plow, the Pentagon's "Peacemaker." The plow gets my vote.

John Updike would probably consider this whole discussion futile. The poet and novelist protests that peace is only "an illusory respite we earn. On both the personal and national level, islands of truce created by balances of terror and potential violence are the best we can hope for."[1] Can he be serious? That's it? Is peace only a pipe dream or at best a temporary halt in armed hostilities, and are peacemakers mere chasers of phantoms?

He may well have it right on military matters. One of the most famous comments on war's futility is George W. Norris's anguished retrospective on World War I, twenty years later, on the eve of World War II.

- We went to war to end militarism, and there is more militarism today than ever before.
- We went to war to make the world safe for

democracy, and there is less democracy today
than ever before.
- We went to war to dethrone autocracy and special privilege, and they thrive everywhere
throughout the world today.
- We went to war to win the friendship of the
world, and other nations hate us today.
- We went to war to purify the soul of America,
and instead we only drugged it.
- We went to war to awaken the American people
to the idealistic concepts of liberty, justice and
fraternity, and instead we awakened them
only to the mad pursuit of money.
- All this, and more, the war brought us. It is our
harvest from what we sowed.[2]

We waged war to create peace, but the direct consequence of World War I was World War II. At least we don't
hear any more boasting that "this is the war to end all
wars," or that "peace is just around the corner." We know
better. Nations come to the negotiating table to rest the
best deal they can get from "the other side." Everyone
loses.

What, then, would Jesus have us do? Just what does a
real peacemaker, the kind he wants his disciples to be, do?
How do you make peace?

You act from strength, not weakness

Militarists are right on this point: Weakness cannot
wage peace. On the international scene, if Sri Lanka or
Nepal were to demand that hostilities cease, who would
listen? When the former Yugoslavia erupted in multiple
civil wars, the whole world looked to America, not Zaire,
to stop the slaughter. Only America could do it. No other
country had the economic and military power to talk *and*
act tough. When the United States government stuttered,

the world groaned. What hope is there for the weak when the strong vacillate?

Closer to home—*at* home, anyone's home—anarchy rules when the head of the house whines, "What do I have to do to get some peace and quiet around here?" If he doesn't know, or won't take decisive action, who will? Who else can?

You want peace? Act from strength, not weakness.

Have you ever wondered what really brought the Yanks home from Vietnam? No one today claims America won. Toward the end of that protracted war the bitter joke was that the U.S. should declare victory and go home. The joke became prophecy. I'm not proposing we should have stayed any longer. Pundits and veterans alike complain we never should have gone in the first place. But once in—so far in—why did we back out? Because the numbers were against us—the human numbers, that is. The war had deteriorated into a head count ("today the enemy lost 135, our side only lost 36"); General Westmoreland kept raising the ante on the number of personnel he had to have. At the peak, he had more than a half million GI's under his command. (Mohammed Ali summed up America's involvement as "white men sending black men to kill yellow men.") An exasperated President Johnson pressed the general: "When we add divisions, can't the enemy add divisions? If so, where does it all end?" And what would happen, he pushed further, if the Communists called for Chinese volunteers? "That's a good question," was Westmoreland's muted reply.[3]

A critical question. China could have supplied an endless stream of troops. In a war of body counts, the Chinese had the strength. America could neither keep pace—nor make peace. In a numbers war, the United States wasn't strong enough. Our will to win was broken.

For a while, the government back home continued to announce a steady string of victories: We were killing more than the enemy was. The once unsuspecting public turned skeptical. In time our suspicions were confirmed: the reports were bogus. Our propaganda scored higher victories than our armies. Karl Kraus's famous axiom never applied more truly: "How is the world ruled and how do wars start? Diplomats tell lies to journalists and then believe what they read."

Today America hates to talk about Vietnam, although the war may have been one of the most educational, because it was the most humbling, periods of our history. Any delusion of American invincibility was shattered. We had tried our strength and found it lacking. We tested our will power and found it wavering. We beat our chest and got beaten.

Today the United States plays a much diminished role as the world's peacekeeper, and the future threatens to shrink us even more. Our debt-ridden economy can't support any protracted peacekeeping missions. We thank God for a shattered Soviet Union and pray no other country will claim its vacated superpower role. We aren't up to another war.

We've learned that if you want to be a peacekeeper, you must be strong—and we don't feel so good.

Jesus obviously does not have military power in mind when he commends peacekeeping to his disciples, but personal strength, spiritual fortitude. "You will receive power when the Holy Spirit comes on you," he promised as he left his disciples (Acts 1:8), and "I am with you always" (Matthew 28:20). You will be strong enough to be a peacemaker. He will see to it.

You make certain everyone wins

In our competitive society, every contest demands a winner (and lots of losers). You know the slogans: "Winner take all." "To the victor go the spoils." "Everybody loves a winner." You also know how to play the game:

"Heads I win, tails you lose." In the Olympic contests, all praise goes to the gold medal winner. Who remembers the also-rans?

But what have the wars of the past century proved beyond rebuttal if not that, in the conflict of nations, eventually everyone loses. This was a conviction deeply held by one of the era's foremost warriors, Dwight Eisenhower. One day Marian Wright Edelman, head of the Children's Defense Fund, found copies of her father's old *Christian Century* magazines on top of the back porch freezer. One was folded to an Eisenhower quotation that her father had underlined. It so moved her she had it made into a poster for her organization.

> Every gun that is made, every warship launched, every rocket fired signifies a theft from those who hunger and are not fed, those who are cold and not clothed. This world in arms is not spending money alone. It is spending the sweat of its laborers, the genius of its scientists, the hope of its children.[4]

What makes President Eisenhower's statement so appealing is its concern for more than the countries at war. His vision transcends national boundaries. American presidents customarily defend their bellicose actions by referring to their responsibility as the nation's leader to protect national security. They mean well; theirs is the viewpoint expected of the Commander in Chief, but it is at the same time one that fosters war. Eisenhower's compassion embraces all people, everywhere. Idealistic? Yes. But this is the idealism essential to peace.

You love your neighbor

During the last couple of decades I've led several tours to the Holy Land. My greatest pleasure on these excursions is introducing first-time visitors to sites that, no matter how much they prepared for the trip, are never exactly what they expected. Bible scenes come alive, but often in surprising ways. No pilgrim returns home quite the same.

Even though I've made multiple trips now, I'm like these first-time visitors in one respect. I'm never quite prepared for the animosity—no, the undisguised hatred—separating Israelis and Palestinians. A family feud that has been fought for thousands of years won't magically disappear in our lifetime, of course. Palestine isn't Camelot. But how I'd love to wave Merlin's magic wand to make peace.

One far greater than Merlin lived his life there. In his day, the enemy was Rome, but before that the dominating names sounded like headliners in today's news: Syria, Egypt, Jordan, and Lebanon. Jesus had no magic wand, either, but in his passion he gave everything to bring peace to his troubled homeland.

His spiritual descendants share his passion. A contemporary example is Elias Chacour, a Palestinian Christian whose family lost their Galilean homes when the new state of Israel was carved out of Palestine. Rather than ruing his people's fate, Chacour has devoted himself to the quest for peace. For that purpose he founded the Prophet Elias Technological High School and College for students of all religious and ethnic backgrounds. Being a peacemaker, he says, "means taking the side of the oppressed, underprivileged, and persecuted without becoming one-sided against the persecutor and the oppressor. If you really want to help the oppressed, since he is always at the mercy of his oppressor, *you have to care for both—convert the oppressor and uplift the oppressed (italics mine).*"[5] It's his way of loving his neighbor.

Have you ever read Jesus' parable of the lost son in Luke 15:11-32 from the father's point of view? Look at it again. There are two sons, the first a typical firstborn, pliable, eager to please, hardworking, and responsible. No way would he leave his father to manage the home place alone. He'd take his orders, shoulder his burden, and accept his fate. He'd be there for his father.

He certainly would not be like his younger brother, restless, ungrateful, profligate. Never could he have behaved like his sibling, demanding his share of the inheritance to squander it in the fast lane. Typical second son.

With two such sons, neither understanding the other, each wrong in his own way, what's a father to do?

He will love them both, and tailor that love to meet each son's needs. So he grants the younger son's request for his inheritance, then eagerly waits for the day he'll wise up. Then he'll celebrate the return of the prodigal. In the meantime, he will enjoy the company of the older son, and affirm him when he doubts his father's affection.

> *"My son," the father said, "you are always with me, and everything I have is yours. But we had to celebrate and be glad, because this brother of yours was dead and is alive again; he was lost and is found."* Luke 15:31, 32

Two sons. One father, who loves them both.

Two nations. One Father, who loves them both. Jesus' injunction to his disciples to be peacemakers isn't naive idealism; it's the love of the Father pleading through the Son for the well-being of all his children everywhere. Blessed are the peacemakers—for they shall be called children of God! They are loved of God and lovers through whom God's love brings peace to all who will receive it.

You act like a child of God

"Blessed are the peacemakers" ends with a prediction: "for they will be called children of God." By whom? Is this only God's nickname for them—or will it catch on here, before they die? Why does Jesus call peacemakers children of God? Let me venture this guess: Peacemakers are children of God because they are so much like the Son of God. Like him,

- They would rather give than take.

Jesus said, "It is more blessed to give than to receive." They have taken him seriously, and found it so.

- They choose to protect instead of passing by. *Like the Good Samaritan, they can't ignore the crying need of another.*
- They share instead of stealing. *In a world where theft is rife, peacemakers will not take what belongs to someone else; rather, they generously share the little they have with those who have less.*
- They defer instead of demanding. *They can let others go first. They can stand while others sit. They can applaud while others take their bows.*
- They turn the other cheek. *Peacemakers almost inevitably suffer for their faith, but the spirit of vengeance is absent. They forgive.*
- They serve the general, rather than their specific, good. *Personal ambition, although undoubtedly a temptation, is not their dominant passion. They are eager to build the kingdom of God on earth.*
- They defend others. *But not themselves. They are too busy to worry about their own feelings.*
- They laugh at themselves but not at others. *Wars are waged by people who take themselves too seriously and others not seriously enough.*
- They refuse to let others tell them what they should think about someone else. *They think— and love—for themselves. As a result, guided by the Holy Spirit, they learn to love without prejudice. They are on everyone's side. They want everyone to win. Thus they bring peace.*

They are becoming like Jesus. Like Jesus, they are doing everything they can to make peace.

That's why they are called—as he said they would be— children of God.

[1]John Updike, *Self-Consciousness*. New York: Alfred A. Knopf, 1989, p. 131.

[2]"After Twenty Years," reprinted in H. E. Fay and M. Frankes, ed., *The Christian Century Reader,* pp. 214, 215.

[3]William Manchester, *The Glory and the Dream*. Boston, Toronto: Little, Brown and Company, 1974, pp. 1312, 1313.

[4]Marian Wright Edelman, *The Measure of Our Success*. Boston: Beacon Press, 1992, p. 77.

[5]*Christianity Today,* March 4, 1996, p. 33.

Rejected for the Right Reasons

Blessed are those who are persecuted
because of righteousness, for theirs is the kingdom
of heaven. Blessed are you when people insult you, persecute
you and falsely say all kinds of evil against you because of me.
Rejoice and be glad, because great is your reward
in heaven, for in the same way they persecuted
the prophets who were before you.
Matthew 5:10-12

The letter to the editor in *Time* magazine a few years ago says it all. The writer waxed indignant about the recorded "Please hold" messages you get on the phone when you're waiting for your call to be transferred. To keep you dangling, a voice periodically breaks into the music to assure that your call is important and your party will be with you any moment now. Probably everyone finds these recordings irritating. For the correspondent, however, "irritating" is too soft a word for what she feels while holding. "This suffering takes endurance if not restraint," she complains.

Suffering. Endurance. Restraint. What words would she use to describe a real problem? Her exaggerated reaction illustrates the resistance Jesus' eighth Beatitude faces in an age like ours. We affluent Westerners can endure anything but discomfort. Every visit to one of the "developing" countries is a reminder that freedom is not universal. In many nations, to admit to being a Christian is to invite persecution, even death. Believers in these closed nations can't bear a cross lightly; they take theirs up daily. Life is hard, martyrdom an ever-present possibility. Their suffering really does take endurance. In that respect they are imitating Jesus, who lived with crescendoing criticism from the beginning of his public ministry until its explosion in full-scale persecution and death.

Isaiah prophesied that the Messiah would be "despised and rejected by men, a man of sorrows, and familiar with suffering." (Isaiah 53:3) The Messiah in turn predicted that his disciples would suffer the same fate:

> "If the world hates you, keep in mind that it hated me first. If you belonged to the world, it would love you as its own. As it is, you do not belong to the world, but I have chosen you out of the world. That is why the world hates you. Remember the words I spoke to you: 'No servant is greater than his master.' If they persecuted me, they will persecute you also. If they obeyed my teaching, they will obey yours also."   John 15:18-20

Not a prospect that would appeal to the masses. Yet of himself as well as of his followers, Jesus would say, "Blessed are those who are persecuted because of righteousness."

Persecuted. Not merely discomforted or inconvenienced, but actively abused. For doing right. As the earliest believers said of themselves, "We must go through many hardships to enter the kingdom of God" (Acts 14:22). Paul warned Timothy, "Everyone who wants to live a godly life in Christ Jesus will be persecuted" (2 Timothy 3:12). The words of Hebrews often come to mind when I'm feeling a little distressed because of criticism or long hours or whatever: "In your struggle against sin, you have not yet resisted to the point of shedding your blood" (12:4). It isn't just sin we struggle against, but sinners, as the preceding verse indicates. "Consider him who endured such opposition from sinful men, so that you will not grow weary and lose heart" (v. 3). Christianity is not for the timid.

This Beatitude bears some looking into.

Persecution promised

Jesus foresaw a future of trouble. He had a cross to face. His disciples after him would confront their own forms of persecution. Consider Paul and Silas, for example, who were cast unceremoniously into the prison at Philippi—for doing good (Acts 16:16-40). Rather than resenting their incarceration, their almost eerie euphoria confounds their keepers. They could have cursed their luck; instead, they pray and sing hymns and entertain their fellow prisoners. This passage doesn't surprise us today, because we have the advantage of reading Paul's reflections on another prison stay. Writing back to his friends in Philippi from his later Roman imprisonment, he could assure them that this latest lockup "has really served to advance the gospel" (Philippians 1:12). His guards and all others who learn of his situation hear that "I am in chains for Christ" (v. 13). He may be temporarily sidelined, but the mission to which he has given his life is advancing, and doing so not *in spite* of but because of his imprisonment. He's not complaining, but rejoicing. He invites his friends to join him.

Like Paul, Peter cautions his friends not to be surprised at the suffering they are enduring; they should "rejoice that you participate in the sufferings of Christ, so that you may be overjoyed when his glory is revealed." They can consider themselves blessed when they are insulted because of their association with Christ, "for the Spirit of glory and of God rests on you" (1 Peter 4:12-14).

So it has been from the first century until now. Jesus' disciples have faced hardship of every kind. Christian history has been written, we are often reminded, in the blood of martyrs.

Contemporary accounts of suffering for Christ's sake prove that our troubles aren't over. Years ago I filed a *Time* article (November 18, 1974) on Christian martyrdom in the African country of Chad, as just one example:

> A black evangelist was sewed up inside a tom-tom and starved to death while drummers pounded incessantly on the skin top. The bodies of several other Christians have been found buried up to their necks in sand, their heads swarming with ants. According to some reports, more than 130 native Protestant pastors and lay church leaders have been assassinated in the land-locked African republic of Chad since last November.

Here is a later one, from *Christianity Today*. The article is entitled, "The Suffering Church." It reads like a numbing travelogue of torture, spotlighting country after country in which Christians are under siege. "Increasingly, Christians are harassed, arrested, interrogated, imprisoned, fined, or killed because of their religious beliefs and practices," the article begins, then takes us around the map:

- Cuba: Pentecostal pastor Orson Vila was imprisoned in May 1995 for conducting "illicit" religious meetings; he remains under house arrest.

- Egypt: Muslim racketeers demand "protection money" from Christian farmers in Upper Egypt; at least two farmers have been murdered after refusing to pay.
- Algeria: Islamic fundamentalist terrorists slit the throats of seven French Trappist monks on May 22.
- Sudan: In August 1995, five Nuban Christian women were sentenced to death for apostasy. In September 1995, ten people were arrested for converting to Christianity.
- Pakistan: In the past year, at least five Christians have died while in police custody. A blasphemy law mandates the death penalty for anyone convicted of blaspheming against the Prophet Muhammad.
- Saudi Arabia: Last December, seven Indian nationals were arrested for conducting private Christmas services. Conversion from Islam to any other religion is a crime punishable by death.
- Iran: Three top evangelical leaders were murdered in 1994. Pastors are interrogated and detained by police. Converts from Islam face imprisonment and torture. Execution is the official penalty for "apostasy."
- Laos: Last year, northern provincial officials began a campaign to close down all known Protestant and Catholic churches. Christians have been forced to sign affidavits renouncing faith and promising to stop all Christian activities.
- Vietnam: At least thirteen Protestants and dozens of Catholic leaders were imprisoned last year because of their religious activities.

- China: Christians in autonomous house churches this year experienced stronger government pressures due to a new campaign that all unsanctioned places of worship be registered.
- North Korea: Religious literature cannot be imported. Missionaries are denied entry, and only three Christian congregations are licensed for twenty-five million people.[1]

David Garrison of Cooperative Services International in Richmond, Virginia, estimates that 250,000 Christians are being martyred annually—in this supposedly enlightened century. In the first four months of 1991 alone, he reported that 300,000 Sudanese Christians were deliberately starved to death by the Islamic government of the Sudan. The deaths could have been avoided. If the Christians had converted to Islam, they would have had access to food and water. They were killed for righteousness' sake.

What the news media and our own travels are teaching us is that American believers, enjoying a certain amount of freedom and protection from persecution, are not typical of the circumstances of Christ's followers worldwide. The average Christian today lives in a developing country, speaks a non-European language, and exists under the threat of murder, imprisonment, torture, or rape.

I have included the journal clippings in this chapter because they are so often not reported in the secular press. It may come as a surprise to most American readers to learn that, in much of the world, Christians are hated. Western Christians are the insulated ones. The majority of Christ's disciples live where noble-sounding terms like "human rights" and "religious liberty" speak of a fantasy world. Their reality is far different.

In light of these conditions, then, we have to ask what Jesus means when he says of the persecuted ones, "theirs is the kingdom of heaven."

They are already in the kingdom of Heaven

Jesus uses the present tense in the Beatitude, and a state of being verb. They already enjoy heavenly relationships, they have received rewards that can't be comprehended by the earthbound, and they value what God values (that is, people above things). They may suffer for a while under the tyranny of some temporal dictator, but their real Lord is above all governments and principalities. They will be law-abiding as far as possible, but they cannot bow the knee to any god. Only to God.

To clarify what this means, let me turn to an unlikely example. I have retained my childhood fascination with Albert Einstein, who died when I was in high school. For the youth of my generation, he represented pure intellectuality. We joked about his casual (sloppy?) dress, his absent-mindedness, and his unruly hair. If one of our fellow students betrayed signs of becoming an academic overachiever, we quickly cut him down with a curt, "Well who do you think you are, anyway, Albert Einstein?" But we deeply admired, though we couldn't pretend to understand, the genius who introduced us to relativity and quantum theory.

My continuing admiration has less to do with physics, though, than with his humility before the great questions of the universe. On April 18, 1955, Einstein died in his sleep at Princeton Hospital. He left on his desk his last incomplete statement, written to honor Israeli Independence Day. Here was one final utterance of the purity of his quest: "What I seek to accomplish is simply to serve with my feeble capacity truth and justice at the risk of pleasing no one."

Here they are, mind and heart conjoined, the search for truth wed to the search for justice. He succeeded in the one more than the other. He himself once noted, "Politics are for the moment. An equation is for eternity." What I admire about him, though, is that his quest never ended, even though the risk cost him dearly. By the time he died, he was considered a back number, pushed to the side of the scientific community. He was tolerated at best, at worst scorned by more sophisticated thinkers as a latter-day Don Quixote, tilting at windmills.

What Einstein did for science ("serve . . . at the risk of pleasing no one"), Christians do for the sake of righteousness—and with the same predictable results. Yet, like Einstein, disciples of Christ do not give up. Our goal is not to hear the applause of our contemporaries but the "Well done" of our Master. We live in a kingdom not limited to this world; we serve a King who cheers us on, even as others ridicule.

The persecuted have
the satisfaction of giving their all

The title of Oswald Chamber's most famous book says it all: *My Utmost for His Highest*. Nothing is more gratifying than giving the most you have to offer to the highest cause there is. It was in this spirit that the apostle Paul wrote to the Romans, "So, as much as in me is, I am ready to preach the gospel" (Romans 1:15, *King James Version*). He couldn't give any more, and he couldn't give to anything better. "For I am not ashamed of the gospel of Christ: for it is the power of God unto salvation to every one that believeth" (v. 16, *King James Version*). Although his commitment would cost him every form of discomfort and persecution, he would not be moved from his course. Nothing else was as satisfying.

Paul's words came to mind when we visited Christians in Kathmandu. We were thrilled to learn of a genuine movement toward Christ among the Nepalese, a country that has long been hostile to the gospel. In 1990 there were approximately twenty-five thousand Christians in the country. By 1996, the number was at least three hundred thousand, meeting in around two thousand churches. We rejoiced to hear these numbers but were saddened to learn of the high price being paid for these conversions. Our host and his wife had been evicted from their home more than a dozen times in the past three years—because they were Christians. New converts were disowned by their families, dismissed from their castes, fired from their jobs. The pastor's broken fingers spoke mutely of one imprisonment, the large scars on his back testified of his beatings. In the countryside, overt persecution continues, even though it has subsided somewhat in the cities. Yet the joy of these believers is irrepressible. They are the persecuted, but they feel blessed.

Theirs is the character of John Bunyan, the Puritan author of *Pilgrim's Progress,* who wrote of his arrest for preaching the gospel: "We might have been apprehended as thieves or murderers or for other wickedness, but blessed be God, it is not so. We suffer as Christians for well-doing, and had better be the persecuted than the persecutors."

Paul, the Nepalese pastors, and hosts of Christian martyrs everywhere have fought, and continue to fight, for the spiritual liberation of all people, regardless of nationality or race. They, too, have acquiesced to imprisonment as a means to a glorious end. They give all that is within them, even if it means their death, because they are serving the very highest good.

Justifiable pride in being persons who can't be silenced

If they boast, the persecuted boast in the Lord (1 Corinthians 1:31). Having no strength of their own, they trust the one in whom they have believed, "convinced that he is able to guard what [they] have entrusted to him for that day" (2 Timothy 1:12). They are like the beleaguered Woodrow Wilson, weakened by his paralytic stroke, fighting a losing battle to lead the United States into the League of Nations, determined to stand by his principles whether he wins or loses. "I would rather fail in a cause that some-day will triumph," he cheered his supporters, "than to win in a cause that I know someday will fail." He might go down to defeat in the immediate battle, but in the war he was waging for worldwide peace he believed his purposes would ultimately prevail.

Paul Tournier, the Swiss Christian psychiatrist whose writings helped so many young ministers a few decades ago, said somewhere that less than 7 percent of the human population have independent minds. It's no wonder there are so few, when you consider how the majority brands and burns them as heretics. But then, it was Edward R. Murrow who always deliberately took the side of heretics against their persecutors, "because the heretics so often proved right in the long run. Dead—but right!"[3]

So the battle is joined between the righteous, the fight-ers for justice and godliness in a unjust, godless world, and their tormentors. Read Paul's catalog of suffering for Christ in 2 Corinthians 11. For Christ he endured every indignity: He was overworked, imprisoned, flogged, exposed and left to die, beaten with lashes and rods, stoned, shipwrecked, adrift at sea, hunted, sleep-deprived, hungry, thirsty, cold, naked, and under severe pressure on behalf of the churches. He was all this and more; but he was never silenced. He was like Sir Andrew Barton in the old Scottish Ballad:

> "I am hurt," Sir Andrew Barton said,
>   "I am hurt, but I am not slain;
> I'll lie me down and bleed awhile,
>   And then I'll fight again."

In addition to everything else, Paul was harassed by something he called his "thorn in my flesh," which drove him to beg God for deliverance. God refused. Instead, he promised Paul, "My grace is sufficient for you, for my power is made perfect in weakness." So Paul perservered, taking "delight in weaknesses, in insults, in hardships, in persecutions, in difficulties" (2 Corinthians 12:8-10). In weakness he discovered *his* strength—not his strength, exactly, but the strength of "him who is able to do immeasurably more than all we ask or imagine, according to his power that is at work within us" (Ephesians 3:20). Through that strength, and because of that strength, he could carry on. He would not be silenced.

The persecuted look forward to the joy that awaits them

The persecuted are like their Lord, enduring the worst because of the best that lies ahead (Hebrews 12:2). As James has written, "Blessed is the man who perseveres under trial, because when he has stood the test, he will receive the crown of life that God has promised to those who love him" (James 1:12).

---

[1]Kim A. Lawton, "The Suffering Church." *Christianity Today*, July 15, 1996.

[2]*Context*, June 15, 1992, p. 6.

[3]A. M. Sperber, *Murrow: His Life and Times*. New York: Freundlich Books, 1986.

10

On Getting What's Coming to You

Come, you who are blessed by my Father;
take your inheritance, the kingdom prepared for you
since the creation of the world.
Matthew 25:34

All of Jesus' Beatitudes aren't collected in the Sermon on the Mount. He speaks to "the blessed ones" in other Scriptures also. This chapter will be a study of Matthew 25:34, where Jesus promises we'll get what's coming to us.

In chapter eight we looked briefly at the prodigal son. Restless under his father's tutelage and eager to drink in life on his own terms, he wanted his share of the inheritance and he wanted it now. Sadly, he didn't want enough. He made a young man's common mistake, dreamed only a young man's dreams. He had no way of knowing what richer treasures lay ahead, riches beyond his imagining. He sacrifices his larger legacy in the impatience of youth. A child's dream is not the adolescent's, nor does ambitious youth lust after old age's legacy. Fortunately, our dreams change as we mature.

I have surprised myself in recent years. Two years ago I took drastic action, doing something I'd once have thought impossible. I began giving away my library. I never counted the volumes, but my holdings at the church covered the four walls and more of my study; then there were the two walls full of Bible study books at home. In addition, I kept an additional small collection in my college office. In the past, every time we moved I gave away boxes full of books, keeping only the "necessary tools." But this time was different. We'd been in Mesa sixteen years and we weren't moving. The giving of books didn't signal a change of address, but a change of heart.

Age is the difference, I suppose. I am older. (At a recent national committee meeting, one of the rising young stars pointed out to the assembled group just how old I'm getting. "Why, Roy's so old," he said, "that if he were a car we'd have to keep a pan under him." The young whippersnapper!) For all my preaching career, I've paid dearly (too dearly, my wife would tell you) to collect these books. "Essential to my trade," I rationalized. Either that, or essential to my ego. At this stage of life, though, the drive to possess has waned. No longer interested in accumulating "things," even things as important as my library, I am seeking a more substantial, more lasting inheritance.

Perhaps I've been influenced more than I was aware by the legacy my father left me. For many years he fretted he wouldn't be able to leave his three children any kind of estate. When he died, we were all surprised that he did have a modest one, enough to leave my sister, brother, and me about ten thousand dollars apiece. True to the family tradition, I almost immediately wiped mine out in a bad investment. Like the prodigal son, I squandered my inheritance.

Only the money, though, which was the least of Dad's legacy. A good role model, he provided an example I've been drawing on all my life; an interesting person, he gave us a host of indelible memories; a caring father, he left his children with a strong sense of having been loved and cheered for; a believer with a modest but real faith, he encouraged belief in God.

That's our real inheritance. It can't be stolen or squandered on a bad investment. I wouldn't trade it for anything else.

But, Jesus says, you and I have another blessing coming, available for the taking now.

In three simple stories in Matthew 25, Jesus prepares his disciples for the future God has made ready for his blessed ones. The key players in each parable act their parts against the backdrop of God's sovereignty. Whether the subject is a wedding, the settling of financial accounts, or the final separation of the saved from the lost, in each instance God acts judiciously. He has known what he's been doing from the beginning, "since the creation of the world." Wise are those who heed Jesus's words. They will be ready.

The first story is of the wise and foolish bridesmaids (25:1-13). It's a one-point sermon, a quietly dramatic tale to pave the way for the moral: "Therefore keep watch, because you do not know the day or the hour." The Bridegroom (Christ) is coming; the diligent will be prepared, the negligent will miss the party. Any bridesmaid who fails to get ready will miss the fun. The parable couldn't be more straightforward.

To insure that we understand what that readiness entails, Jesus tells the story of the talents (25:14-30). Once again, he turns his disciples' attention to the future, to his

return when, without apparent warning, he will appear
and ask his stewards to turn in their books for the audit.
The moral of the tale is simple also: Be faithful in using
God's investment (now) so that when the books are settled
(then) your stewardship of his resources will show a handsome profit.

The parable of the sheep and the goats wraps up Jesus'
trilogy on the final judgment. Once more the Lord drives
home a constant theme in his teaching: blessings are for
the benevolent. This is the passage we'll study more
closely, because it contains one of Jesus' Beatitudes. In fact,
it yields additional Beatitudes.

Blessed are the unself-conscious.

*For I was hungry and you gave me something to eat, I was
thirsty and you gave me something to drink, I was a stranger
and you invited me in, I needed clothes and you clothed me, I
was sick and you looked after me, I was in prison and you came
to visit me.*   Matthew 25:35, 36

According to Caroline Walker Bynum, the early church
father Tertullian was of the opinion that we won't chew in
Heaven. Our resurrection bodies won't need physical sus-
tenance. We'll still need teeth, though, because otherwise
we would look funny. Without them we would be too self-
conscious. Cyprian of Carthage, another early church
leader, had his own views on the subject. He discouraged
women from wearing face powder in this life; they don't
want to run the risk that God might fail to recognize them
when they appear powderless in the next.[1]

What *are* we going to look like in Heaven? We don't
know any more than Tertullian or Cyprian knew, of
course. Whatever form our body takes, we won't need any
mirrors in our heavenly house. Primping will be out of
fashion there, as will parading our religiosity to impress
people (Matthew 6:1-18). On this subject, Tertullian is

wrong. We won't be self-conscious in Heaven, and it's really inappropriate on earth. As those on the Master's right demonstrate, genuine compassion displays such ease in giving and grace in tending the needy that it can't even remember doing it.

Blessed are the proactive

Look at the verbs: You *fed* me, *gave* me drink, *invited* me in, *clothed* me, *looked* after me, *visited* me. You saw my plight and acted. You didn't wait to be asked. The initiative was yours. You weren't trying to be "religious." You weren't even thinking about God at the time; you certainly weren't trying to score points with him. You just reached out as one human being to another. Ironically, when you were *feeling* least religious, God was quite aware of what you were doing.

Putting the three stories together, we are to understand that Jesus desires disciples who are aware that the Lord could return at any time (vv. 1-13), who are good stewards of the resources God has provided (vv. 14-30), and who look for opportunities to help others in need. They do good deeds that in and of themselves seem less religious than humane; they are acts of kindness that should be routine among human beings.

What a different concept of religion this is. The Lord has nothing to say in this chapter about preparing for Judgment Day through burnt sacrifices or the observance of holy days or holding the proper doctrines.

Blessed are those who can see the little people

I tell you the truth, whatever you did for one of the least of these brothers of mine, you did it for me.   Matthew 25:40

Jesus is as concerned about the "least of these brothers" as he is about the greatest. No one is to be ignored.

Dr. Paul Brand has inspired countless admirers with his

mission work among lepers, who are the easiest of all to overlook. For centuries they have been the "least." One of Dr. Brand's patients, Sadan, once told him, "I am happy that I had the disease leprosy, Dr. Brand." The good physician looked incredulous. Sadan explained, "Without leprosy I would have spent all my energy trying to rise in society. Because of it, I have learned to care about the little people." When he heard this, Dr. Brand thought of Helen Keller's famous words, "I am grateful for my handicap, for through it I found my world, my self, and my God."[2]

One little person is the girl in the well-traveled joke who reads Psalm 23: "Surely good Mrs. Murphy shall follow me all the days of my life." Her reading was righter than she knew. Don't we Christians testify that "goodness and mercy" have actually followed us around, all dressed up like a human being? As a child, in my formative teens, as a struggling young adult, through my most productive years, and now as I move into my seventh decade, God's goodness and mercy are still my companions, usually incarnated in the many Mrs. Murphys who've blessed my life, but almost as often as Mr. Murphy or one of their many offspring.

It isn't always easy to concentrate in a discussion with the Murphys because the subject, especially if you've been talking about yourself, inevitably changes. They're not just concerned about *your* welfare, these Murphys, but about the children, the handicapped, the oddballs, the aging, the victimized. Thank God for the Murphys in our church. They will not allow us to be satisfied that we've done enough to tear down the barriers that prevent the blind, the deaf, the abused, the mentally and emotionally disadvantaged from finding their way into and feeling at home among God's people. The Murphys won't let us gossip about, or, what's worse, ignore the alcoholic, the drug-addicted, the victims of vicious diseases and equally vicious human predators. They wonder what more can be done for the aging, the lonely, the fatherless. Is there any-one their restless eyes don't see?

If you raise a point that maybe the church has collected a pretty unsavory amalgam of sinners, the Murphys immediately remind you of the church at Corinth. "Aren't you grateful for Corinth?" they'll ask. Their point is that the church in that city was populated by *Corinthians*, if you please. And everyone knows what Corinthians were like: Ethnics, merchants, idolaters, prostitutes, charismatics, prudes, sexual profligates, the quite wealthy and the very poor, the whole and the broken. A veritable kaleidoscope of sinners lived in that wicked city. Corinth was famous for them. People traveled from far and wide to look at them. In Athens and Rome, playwrights paraded them on stage for the titillation of the voyeurs in the audience. And some of these Corinthians came to church. The Murphys took them in, and the apostle Paul dubbed them saints. It didn't matter if their skin hue was darker than theirs and their secrets even darker. If they limped or they squinted or they scratched themselves in public, the Murphys weren't turned off.

Goodness and mercy. For the little people.

Blessed are those for whom Heaven has begun

Take your inheritance, the kingdom prepared for you since the creation of the world.   Matthew 25:34

This parable is about Heaven. We'll return to this sub-ject again in chapter 12, but for now let's speculate a bit. What do you suppose these "sheep" are going to do in eternity? Scriptural glimpses of Heaven are few, and the pictures they give us are tantalizing at best. Surely the Lord won't mind our speculating a bit.

Maya Angelou, who often captures the anguish of the African-American experience in her poetry, has some pretty definite ideas of what Heaven will be like—or ought to be. In one of my favorites among her poems she tells the preacher not to promise her streets of gold or free milk. Paradise for her would be where she can find loyal families and nice strangers—and jazz![3]

She doesn't have to worry. Oh, I'm not certain about the jazz—a friend of mine is certain there'll be a steady diet of Bach—but for sure she will find some nice strangers—the Murphys will be there.

You know they'll be there, because it is to them that Jesus says, "Come, you who are blessed by my Father; take your inheritance, the kingdom prepared for you since the creation of the world."

But what will the Murphys do there, these people who spent an earthly lifetime looking around and looking out for people who needed them? Do you remember this old Negro spiritual?

> "Sit down, brother."
> "Can't sit down."
> "Sit down, brother."
> "Can't sit down."
> "Sit down, brother."
> "Can't sit down. I just got to Heaven
>   And I can't sit down!"

I always thought it meant that in Heaven we'd be so excited to be there we'd be dancing and singing and praising God. No silent meditation for us there. This would be celebration time! That is what the spiritual's about, undoubtedly. But I'm wondering if there isn't more to the song, especially if the Murphys are doing the singing. They spent all their preparing-for-Heaven time serving: Visiting the prisons, nursing the sick, assisting the poor, and looking out for strangers. They never confined their religion to sitting or kneeling or studying or praying. Their whole bodies were busy, from the eyes that spotted the need, to the tongue that spoke a word of comfort, to the hands that served, to the feet that took them there. They always felt their best when they were up and doing. Heaven won't be Heaven for them if they have to sit down. They'll be singing their praises with the other saints gathered around the throne, but they'll probably be sneaking an occasional glance around to see whether anyone needs anything!

It's a habit they learned from Jesus. He was the one who spotted the beggar in the temple, the man everyone else had overlooked. When cranky adults would have ushered the little children away from him, he invited them closer. He could feel the power go out of him when a sick woman touched his clothes. For the most part, he taught goodness and mercy by example, but on one remarkable occasion he let everyone know that his ministry was theirs also.

When he raised Lazarus from the tomb, the Lord said two amazing things. First, to Lazarus. His friend had already been put away, out of sight. He smelled. "Lazarus," Jesus called to him in a voice that would be obeyed, "come out!" I want you here where you belong, with the family, among the living.

Lazarus arose, breathing again but badly handicapped. He couldn't walk well; his feet were bound. He couldn't talk right, either; his face was distorted behind the cloth, his tongue thick, his words unintelligible. He was back from the land of the dead, but not yet ready for full conversation with living. He was, at this point, like one of the little people.

So Jesus said the second amazing thing, this time to the bystanders: [You] "Take off the grave clothes and let him go." Now *you* must become involved. I can bring the dead and disadvantaged and different to life again, but you must free them and feed them and welcome them into the embrace of my Father's family.

That's your job. It always has been. If you choose to accept it, one day you will "take your inheritance!"

[1]Caroline Walker Bynum, "The Resurrection of the Body in Western
    Christianity 200-1336" (Columbia University Press) Context, May 1,
    1995, pp. 3, 4.
[2]Dr. Paul Brand and Philip Yancey, *Pain: The Gift Nobody Wants*. New
    York: Harper Collins, Zondervan, 1993, pp. 301, 302.
[3]Maya Angelou, "Preacher, Don't Send Me," *The Poetry of Maya Angelou*.
    New York: Quality Paperback Book Club, 1993, pp. 264, 265.

11

Of Giving and Blessing

It is more blessed to give than to receive.
Acts 20:35

*Now that you know these things,
you will be blessed if you do them.*
John 13:17

*Ill fares the land, to hastening ills a prey,
Where wealth accumulates, and men decay.*
Oliver Goldsmith, "The Deserted Village"

They could almost serve as the epitaph for America, couldn't they, these words from Goldsmith's "The Deserted Village"? Pick up any news magazine, listen to any television commentator. They're all bemoaning America's fate. Our land is sick, the diseases are multiplying.

And the source of the plague is money. In 1957, when economist John Kenneth Galbraith described the United States as *The Affluent Society,* America's per person income, in today's dollars, was less than $8 thousand. Today it's more than $16 thousand. But every study confirms we are more unhappy than ever. You don't need this preacher to tell you: the state of blessedness doesn't depend on the amount of money you have.

It's a lesson Miss Oseola McCarty learned well. Not that she ever had much money. She slaved for decades to earn a meager fifty cents a load doing laundry for families in Hattiesburg, Mississippi. Even on that pittance the thrifty lady managed to squirrel away a bit every week at the local bank. When she retired, well past the standard retirement age, she got around to asking the banker how much money she had in her account.

"Two hundred fifty thousand dollars," was his reply.

The laundry lady, now in her eighties, was in shock. What was she to do with such an estate? "I had more than I could use in the bank. I can't carry anything away from here with me, so I thought it was best to give it to some child to get an education."

Always self-effacing, the unmarried Miss McCarty had simple needs, but her heart was big. She gave $150 thousand to nearby University of Southern Mississippi to help young people attend college. "It's more blessed to give than to receive," she tells reporters. "I've tried it!"[1]

The whole nation, once we learned of her generosity, applauded. "Such rare generosity," we murmured, only vaguely aware she was merely applying one of Jesus' Beatitudes. This one isn't found in the four Gospels. We wouldn't even know about it if the famous preacher, the apostle Paul, hadn't casually mentioned it in his sermon to the elders of the Ephesian church (Acts 20:35). "In everything I did," he challenged them, "I showed you that by this kind of hard work we must help the weak, remembering the words the Lord Jesus himself said: 'It is more blessed to give than to receive.'"

I wonder whether this saying of Jesus was handed down from the night of Judas's betrayal, when Jesus got up from the supper table and washed his disciples' feet. It was an incredible lesson in servanthood. He was taking over the job of a household's lowliest servant—an unthinkable, a humiliating self-abasement for a rabbi. Peter would have none of it. "No," he protested, "you shall never wash my feet" (John 13:8).

You can't blame Peter. Jesus' conduct was unseemly, to say the least. A master never stooped before his disciple. To take a towel and water basin and clean dirty feet—who ever heard of such a thing? Peter was impulsive, but at least he knew his protocol. Never, Lord.

But Jesus washed his feet all the same, and those of the other disciples. Only when he had dried his hands and returned to the table did he tell them what he was up to:

> "You call me 'Teacher' and 'Lord,' and rightly so, for that is what I am. Now that I, your Lord and Teacher, have washed your feet, you also should wash one another's feet. I have set you an example that you should do as I have done for you. I tell you the truth, no servant is greater than his master, nor is a messenger greater than the one who sent him. Now that you know these things, you will be blessed if you do them." John 13:13-17

More blessed to give than receive. Is it possible that Jesus' simple Beatitude could hold the answer to our nation's increasing unhappiness? For the social ills that are tearing us apart? For the misery you and I nurture in our hearts because no one, absolutely no one, treats us the way we deserve?

Before receiving the blessing that giving affords, we have to learn a few basic lessons. Giving doesn't come naturally, at least to people like me. It's especially hard if we haven't learned some basic truths.

What we're giving isn't ours in the first place

This is the first essential truth. When we give, we're not giving up anything that's ours anyway. An old favorite story illustrates the difference this perception makes. A left-leaning, small-town politician was making a speech about the importance of sharing wealth. He didn't mean exactly what Jesus had in mind, since Jesus finds the blessing in voluntarily giving, not in the government's method of extracting wealth, often against our will. This politician, an advocate of the extraction method, spotted someone he knew in the audience. "Mr. Jones, if you had three Cadillacs, wouldn't you give up one of them so we could gather the kids and take them to school during the week?"

The man replied, "Sure I would."

Working up a head of steam, the politician continued, "And if you had $3 million, wouldn't you give up $1 million of it so we could put a roof over people's heads and make sure they had food to eat?"

"Sure," the man replied again.

"And Mr. Jones, if you had three hogs—"

"Now just wait a minute here!" the man interrupted. "I've got three hogs!"

He has—and he hasn't, at least not according to the Bible. God owns it all, "for every animal of the forest is [his], and the cattle on a thousand hills" (Psalm 50:10). Jones has temporary custody of his three hogs, but they don't belong to him. Like the men in Jesus' parable of the ten talents (Matthew 25:14-30), Mr. Jones is a steward who one day will give an accounting of what he did with someone else's hogs.

Seen in this light, the scriptural standard of returning a tithe (the first 10 percent) to God seems much less painful than if we are giving up something that is really our own. The tithing principle recognizes everything we have as God's, and since he has asked for the first tenth, it's only right that he should receive it. Otherwise we really are, as

Malachi 3:8, 9 charges, robbing God.

Ron Sider would have us go beyond the tithe, if we really want to make a difference in the world. He recommends we decide on the standard of living that is right for us and then tithe on that amount. Then out of every thousand dollars of additional income we earn, we should raise our contributions by 5 percent more. With this arrangement, once we have reached $18 thousand above our chosen standard, we can give away 100 percent of all our additional income. We wouldn't want that money to just pile up anyway, since it doesn't belong to us. The rightful Owner might frown on our skimming off such a high cut as the management fee. It reduces the return on his investment.[2]

You will want to work out your own scheme of giving. The important thing to remember is this: They aren't your hogs.

We are giving only what was intended to be given, anyway

The reason God gave you the hogs in the first place is so that you could use them for the benefit of other people. That's why it is in giving, not in saving, that the blessing is found. You are cooperating with God when you give, thwarting his will if you don't.

My traveling companions and I witnessed this cooperation in action when we worshiped with the Nepalese Christians in Kathmandu. More than two hundred believers were there. The service had already stretched to nearly two and a half hours and was coming to a close when the pastor told the congregation of a tragedy that had indirectly struck their church. The son of the man who drove the church's station wagon had fallen off a roof two days earlier and was still in a coma. The father had gone immediately to the distant town to be with his son. Living like most of the Nepalese from day to day, he had no money for the journey or for his son's expenses. Immediately after the pastor told the congregation of the man's plight, he prayed the benediction. The members spontaneously began singing as they left the building—by way of the open sack in front of the pulpit into which they placed their second offering of the morning. These were very poor people, giving and giving again, singing and praising God because they could help someone in need. An outsider would have wondered at their joy. The visiting Americans got in line with them. Some dollars made their way among the rupees that morning, and some foreign tongues joined the Nepalese singing. We were giving away our money, with gladness.

A letter to the editor of *Time* (November 8, 1993, p. 11) castigates Michael Jordan for his premature retirement from basketball—and in the process gives a pretty good stewardship lesson. Christopher G. Janus, of Wilmette, Illinois, strongly disapproves of Jordan's stated reason for retiring ("I have reached the pinnacle—I don't have anything else to prove"). Jordan has no right to retire now, Janus opines in his remarkable letter:

> Michael Jordan, with his God-given talent, hard work and dedication, has become the world's foremost athlete. His fans have made him a role model for children and a goodwill ambassador to the world. Basketball has made him a very wealthy man. With his privileges and accomplishments come important responsibilities: to the game, to his championship teammates and to his business associates—and, yes, even to the Almighty, who gave him his great talent. It's a cop-out for him to say he no longer has a motivation to play. A great, gifted sportsman should quit, not because he wants to, but because his body gives out and he has to. Jordan has hardly reached that point.

However much he may want more time to play golf, however admirable it is for him to want to spend more time taking his children to the playground, his responsibilities as a hero and role model are vastly more important.

Strong language! As far as Mr. Janus is concerned, those aren't Jordan's hogs! God gave him the talent, which he nurtured with hard work and dedication. As a result, Michael Jordan has unique opportunities to do good and he should be doing it as long as he can.

For Mr. Janus, it is not only more blessed to give than to receive, it is a divine duty!

Giving strengthens the giver and blesses the receiver

One evening in Kathmandu our group ate dinner with Sundar and Sarita Thapa, leaders of the church we were visiting. Sundar has devoted his ministry to planting churches and now supervises 120 of them, mostly in the western half of Nepal. This very poor country had depressed us with its nearly insuperable problems. What could be done to overcome the extreme poverty of the masses, the rampant disease, the filth, the reign of monkeys and cows valued so much more than human life? We had turned in disgust from the rituals and incense of the Hindu and Buddhist temples to find a warm welcome in the embrace of the church. There we saw rooms that the church had dedicated for the homeless. We met the orphaned children the church was caring for. We attended the pastors' conference (a combination lectureship/pep rally) and heard the exhortations to do even more good works. What a contrast in spirit: On the one hand, temple worshipers looking out for their own salvation while ignoring the plight of their countrymen; on the other, Christians whose very worship called them to use everything God has given them to do their countrymen good.

On the outside, weakness and apathy. On the inside of the church, increasing strength and determination.

Two or three times Sarita, who was sitting across from me at dinner one evening, casually mentioned the people's tithes. Finally I asked, "Sarita, do all the Christians tithe?" "Oh yes," she assured me, then went on at length to tell me how the tithes enabled the church to help needy people. These Christians earned no more money than the pittance their neighbors earned, yet they all had enough to care for their own needs and give to others as well. As a result, the church was growing and the Christians were becoming stronger.

Jacob Needleman, the "money philosopher," says that "money is a way of speaking about the human condition."[3] We express the meaning we have found in life through our use of money. For some people, life is hell, which Needleman defines as "the state in which we are barred from receiving what we truly need because of the value we give to what we merely want." In Nepal, we experienced a touch of Heaven, as Christians whose possessions were few felt rich enough to give and then give again. They had so little—and yet they had everything. Needleman says it right: They had spoken about the human condition.

They made me think of John Wesley, whose giving was legendary. By the time he died, it is reported that he lived on the tithe and gave the other 90 percent to further the Lord's work. As a result, it was said he "died leaving behind nothing but his Bible, his horse, and the Methodist Church." He had expressed himself. He would love and serve and save, if it took everything he had.

If, on the other hand, I store my wealth in bigger barns, you know what I feel about the human condition—nothing. I'm too absorbed in myself to worry about you. I deserve. My desires must be served. That's enough.

Jesus warned that we can't have it two ways. Either we

will serve God or we will serve Mammon (Money), which is another way of serving ourselves. Dietrich Bonhoeffer says that's because our hearts have room for only one "all-embracing devotion." Richard Foster adds, "What we must recognize is the seductive power of mammon. Money has power, spiritual power, to win our hearts. Behind our coins and dollar bills or whatever material form we choose to give to our money are spiritual forces. It is the spiritual reality behind money that we want so badly to deny. . . . Mammon asks for our allegiance in a way that sucks the milk of human kindness out of our very being."[4]

Sometimes I wish I could preach the way Billy Sunday did. The famous evangelist threw himself into a sermon the way he used to go after his boxing opponents in the ring. Some subjects especially drew his wrath. One of them was the idolatrous love of money. "Money is as truly a god for some people as if they prayed to ten-dollar gold pieces," he fulminated.

> Oh, we are making money in America by the bucketfuls, but we are going to hell in car-lots on excursion rates! Oh, the magic of money! Oh, the rush for money! Oh, the counting of money! Oh, the jealousy of money! Oh, the lying for money. Oh, the stealing for money! Oh, the murder for money! The adultery for money! The gambling for money! Selfishness for money! Oh, the loneliness of the man that has lost all but his money! Oh, the loneliness of the man who has nothing but money! The fellow that has no money is poor; the fellow who has nothing but money is poorer still.[5]

Sunday pommels his subject more vigorously than Foster, but the two agree that the money in our hand talks for us. Where it goes expresses who or what really matters to us, what we really believe, what or whom we will serve: Self, Mammon, fellow human beings, God.

God loves a cheerful giver

"God loves a cheerful giver,"
    As stewardship chairman will vouch,
But contributions are also welcome
    Even if the giver's a grouch.
          —George O. Ludcke

Someone clipped Ludcke's lines from a newspaper and handed them to me one Sunday morning, undoubtedly to cheer me up a little. A discouraging aspect of ministry is the way pastors are badgered for money. My old preacher used to keep a box in the corner to show church members how many appeals the church received a month. Good causes, worthy projects all. I'd have to keep a trunk to hold the ones I receive. And I add to the pile. As a college president whose school depends on voluntary donations for our survival, I regularly solicit gifts. David McKenna, a former university and seminary president, has studied the high-pressure tactics of certain fund-raisers. Pictures of babies with bloated bellies no longer raise the dollars they used to, he observes. More dramatic means have to be applied now to "stimulate the gifts."

Thus, raising the score follows a predictable process. Idealism rules in the beginning, with a simple statement of the needs of the ministry. As the program expands, the time and space given to fund appeals also expand. The initial plea is usually gentle. "Give me money to show your love." Further expansion and a tight budget will add a new dimension to the appeal, "Give me money to get God's blessing," implying the assurance of answered prayer, personal success, and economic prosperity. If a cash crisis comes, however, the fund-raiser can always appeal to loyalists. "Give me money to save my ministry."

However, crisis after crisis can dull that appeal as well. So, as desperation dominates a ministry and escalates the beginning, it is not unusual to hear the veiled threat, "Give me money to save your soul." Then delusions of grandeur take over.[6]

I thank God for the organizations in which I've served. They've never resorted to such ruses. But after working with so many charitable causes over the years, I can assure you that not only God loves a cheerful giver. So do these charities!

God loves an impulsive giver

Wayne Watts says that while he was writing his little book, *The Gift of Giving,* God convicted him to begin giving every time he went to church. Up to then he had been giving the church a monthly check, based on his annual income. He did experience the joy of giving, he said, but the act of making his gift was divorced from worship. The Scripture that inspired him to change was Deuteronomy 16:16, "No man should appear before the Lord empty-handed." So he began to offer something whenever he attended worship, writing a check so he could keep a record of it. If he didn't have a check handy, he gave cash. He tried to keep a tally of the cash, but then, he said, God convicted him again: "You do not need to keep up with the amount of cash. Give to me simply out of a heart of love, and see how much you enjoy the service." He did—and his joy increased.[7]

Nothing dampens your worship quite like a calculating spirit. One reason for not letting your left hand know what your right hand is doing (Matthew 6:3) is so that your impulse to give won't be stifled by fiscal conniving. Give, instead, in the spirit of the Christians Paul praises. "Out of the most severe trial, their overflowing joy and their extreme poverty welled up in rich generosity" (2 Corinthians 8:2). Theirs was the joy we witnessed in Kathmandu.

We'll let the last word on this subject be a child's. Her minister strongly appealed for a sacrificial offering on behalf of the cause he was promoting. At his urging, many came forward to present their love offerings.

One of them was the little girl with a disability who hobbled along at the end of the line. When she reached the offering plate, she pulled a ring from her finger, placed it on the table and made her way back up the aisle.

After the service an usher was sent to bring her to the preacher's study.

"My dear, I saw what you did. It was beautiful. But the response of the people has been so generous that we have enough to take care of the need. We don't feel right about keeping your treasured ring, so we have decided to give it back to you."

She shook her head vigorously in refusal. "You don't understand. I didn't give my ring to you. I gave it to God."[8]

[1]Letter to the congregation, Rob Clark, First Christian Church, Tarpon Springs, FL, May 23, 1996.
[2]Richard J. Foster, *Money, Sex and Power*. San Francisco: Harper and Row, 1985, p. 74.
[3]Bill Moyers, *A World of Ideas*. New York, et al: Doubleday, 1990, p. 165.
[4]Foster, *Money, Sex and Power*, p. 26.
[5]Quoted in Douglas W. Frank, *Less than Conquerors*. Grand Rapids: Eerdmans Publishing Company, 1986, pp. 215, 216.
[6]David L. McKenna, "Financing the Great Commission," *Christianity Today Institute*, May 15, 1987, p. 27.
[7]Wayne Watts, *The Gift of Giving*. Colorado Springs: Navpress, 1982, pp. 35, 36.
[8]*God's Vitamin "C" for the Spirit*, compiled by Kathy Collard Miller and D. Larry Miller. Lancaster, Pennsylvania: Starburst Publishers, 1996, p. 265.

12

What a Way to Go

Blessed are the dead who die
in the Lord from now on.
Revelation 14:13

Earlier in this century, a Greenland Eskimo was taken
on an American expedition to the North Pole. As a reward
for faithful service on the trek, he was brought to New
York City for a visit. He had never seen anything like it.
The tall buildings piercing the skyline, the little rooms that
rose vertically to the top of them, the display windows
bursting with garments and furniture and trinkets he had
never imagined. He was filled with awe. He could hardly
wait to return to his native village, where he told stories of
those buildings that rose to the face of the sky and of street
cars, which he described as houses that moved along a

trail with people living in them as they moved. He told of
mammoth bridges, artificial lights, and all the other daz-
zling phenomena of the great metropolis. His neighbors'
response surprised him as much as the city sights had.
They stared coldly and walked away. They didn't believe
him. What he described was impossible. They dubbed him
Sagdluk, "the liar." In time, they even forgot his original
name. He was known—to his shame—as "The Liar" until
he died.

When Knud Rasmussen undertook his expedition
from Greenland to Alaska he took along an Eskimo
named Mitek, "Elder Duck." Mitek visited Copenhagen
and New York and his discoveries closely paralleled
Sagdluk's, whose tragedy he remembered. He decided it
would be to his advantage not to tell the whole truth. He
told only stories that his people could grasp. He
described how he and Dr. Rasmussen maintained a
Kayak on the banks of a great river, and how each morning they paddled out for their hunting. Most of his
adventures he kept to himself. In the eyes of his countrymen, Mitek was a very honest man. His neighbors
treated him with rare respect.

How, then, shall we talk about Heaven? Many of our
villagers are already convinced nothing like it exists. What
can we tell them that they will believe? When we die, they
are convinced, we are dead. Period. Will they believe the
Bible's report? Can they accept, for example, Revelation
14:13, which contains this wonderful Beatitude:

> Then I heard a voice from heaven say, "Write: Blessed are the
> dead who die in the Lord from now on."
> "Yes," says the Spirit, "they will rest from their labor, for
> their deeds will follow them."

If our fellow villagers have trouble with this Beatitude,
what will they say of a more elaborate description of the
land none of us has seen?

Then I heard what sounded like a great multitude, like the
roar of rushing waters and like loud peals of thunder, shouting:
   "Hallelujah! For our Lord God Almighty reigns.
   Let us rejoice and be glad and give him glory!
   For the wedding of the Lamb has come,
      and his bride has made herself ready.
   Fine linen, bright and clean, was given her to wear."
   (Fine linen stands for the righteous acts of the saints.)
   Then the angel said to me, "Write: 'Blessed are those who are
invited to the wedding supper of the Lamb!'" And he added,
"These are the true words of God."   *Revelation 19:6-9*

Blessed are those who die in the Lord . . . who are
invited to the wedding supper of the Lamb. Perhaps our
villagers can be persuaded to believe this much, that death
is not to be feared, at least not by those whom the Lord
has called.[1]

Maybe Ray Payne's testimony would help them. When
Joy and I visited Ray in the hospital, he had just days to
live. Pneumonia was rapidly claiming his life. Calls like this
one should be brief. We stayed too long, enjoying being
with Ray, his wife, Betty, and their granddaughter Christy,
home from college to see her granddad for the last time.

As another friend from church arrived, we quickly said
our good-byes, knowing that she would pray with them
before leaving. We did not want to tire Ray any more than
necessary. Betty followed us into the hallway with us.
There she could alert us to the gravity of Ray's condition
out of earshot. She said Ray had told her a little earlier that
he wanted to die. He was not depressed nor suicidal; he
wasn't giving up in despair. He trusted the Lord's grace.
He believed his time had come, and he was worn out.
More importantly, he was looking ahead.

While we were still talking together, Alice came to tell
us Ray wanted us to come to his bedside for prayer. As
we circled, I noted that he seemed stronger than he did
when we left just a few minutes earlier. With our hands

clasped around the bed, Ray removed his mask (he was breathing 100 percent oxygen) and, not waiting for anyone else, he prayed vigorously. He didn't ask a thing for himself; his prayer was for us. I was so moved I had difficulty speaking when my turn came. It was, to borrow a term from Revelation, a Hallelujah moment. Fully in charge of himself, Ray was preparing to cast off his natural and put on his spiritual body, as Paul describes death in 1 Corinthians 15 (verses 41-55). Or, again using the words of Revelation, he was leaving for the "wedding supper of the Lamb."

Ray's funeral was held a few days later. Family and friends assembled. If you had been there but didn't understand English, you'd have thought you were in a routine worship service. There was no weeping and wailing and gnashing of teeth. A few tears, much singing, and upbeat words from the Scripture. And the words of the presiding minister told the people what they already knew: "Blessed are the dead who die in the Lord."

Blessed forever

The Scriptures begin and end in blessing. At the creation, "God blessed them [the new creation] and said, 'Be fruitful and increase in number and fill the water in the seas, and let the birds increase on the earth'" (Genesis 1:22). And then, after creating humanity in his own image, God blessed them and urged them to fill the earth and subdue it, ruling over "the fish of the sea and the birds of the air and over every living creature that moves on the ground" (1:28).

In his concern for his created ones, "God blessed the seventh day and made it holy, because on it he rested from all the work of creating that he had done" (Genesis 2:3).

In creation God blesses, and, as we have already read in Revelation, in conclusion God blesses. But of what does it consist, this blessing he has prepared?

Heaven consists of surprises

The English language fails us when we try to describe Heaven. Human imagination can't grasp it. "No eye has seen, no ear has heard, no mind has conceived what God has prepared for those who love him" (1 Corinthians 2:9). Even an experienced preacher hesitates before addressing the subject, aware he's venturing beyond where his experience and vocabulary can carry him. Those who have gone before are silent on the subject: Elijah sent back no report, Lazarus seems to have left no record. Even Jesus, during his forty-day postresurrection sojourn, bent his efforts to insure the success of his disciples' earthly ministry rather than relate his experience in death. So we are left to wonder—and trust.

Of one fact we can be certain, though. Only God knows for sure who'll be at the wedding feast. Even the guest list will be surprising, at least according to this poem printed by "Dear Abby." She said one of her readers sent it to her, and he said it came from a leaflet published by St. Catharine's in Ontario, Canada.

Take These Lines to Heart
I dreamed death came to me one night
　　and Heaven's gates flew open wide.
With kindly grace St. Peter came and
　　ushered me inside.
There to my astonishment were friends
　　I had known on Earth.
Some I had labeled as unfit and some
　　of little worth.
Indignant words flew to my lips;
　　words I could not set free,
For every face showed stunned surprise—
　　no one expected me.

In chapter ten we studied Jesus' parable of the last judgment. Surprise is the dominant element in that story.

According to Jesus, we'll not only be surprised at the guest list, but surprised by the reasons for their being selected. "Lord, when did we see thee?"

W. C. Fields died on Christmas Day in 1946. A visitor who came to see him during his last hospitalization expressed astonishment at catching him reading the Bible. "Just looking for loopholes," he deadpanned.

He was hoping to be surprised. Surprises there will be, but no loopholes.

Heaven promises joy

C. S. Lewis *was* surprised by what he discovered when he abandoned his atheism for the promises of the Christian faith. *Surprised by Joy* is the title he gives his autobiography. As far as Lewis is concerned, joy is the experience of the Christian on earth and joy is the serious business of Heaven, where the world's makers of misery will be powerless to spoil the party. There, at the wedding feast, joy will prevail.

There was joy in Ray Payne's hospital room. Joy prevailed at his funeral. If the Scriptures are to be believed, he was greeted in Heaven by joy. "Welcome to the wedding feast. We're so glad you came. You will be, too."

Heaven offers more of the same, only better

Every survey on the subject confirms America's near-universal belief in Heaven. Yet, when you look at the statistics regarding church attendance, you wonder what people are thinking. They aviod worship, they are turned off by religious people, they are almost totally ignorant of God's Word, and they have only the fuzziest notions about God himself. Scriptures about Heaven, however, picture its inhabitants spending all their time worshiping before the throne of God, reveling in his presence and in the company of all the other saints assembled there, thoroughly enjoying just hanging around their maker and redeemer. If people can't stand these things on earth, what makes them think they're going to find Heaven so appealing?

I raise the question because of a long-standing conviction. When you read everything Jesus has to say about the kingdom of Heaven, you have trouble sometimes distinguishing whether he's talking about the kingdom *of* Heaven (on earth) or the kingdom *in* Heaven. It's as if, for him, the kingdom to come will be more of the same; what gives greatest pleasure on earth will be intensified in Heaven.

That's why I wonder how people who ignore the kingdom on earth can expect their after-death experience to be so wonderful.

The great German author Goethe takes a little different tack on the subject. Not one to go gently into death, he concentrated his waning powers until they blazed with rekindled energy and intellectual violence. He had no doubt he would live beyond the grave. He didn't base his conviction on any word of the Lord. To someone of his powers, whose indefatigable labors would bear him right up to the brink of death, "nature is obliged" to assign "another form of existence when the present form is no longer able to contain my spirit."[2]

You can accuse Goethe of many things. Humility isn't one of them.

There's contagion in his defiance. His nineteenth-century boast, "Nature is obliged" spread to the twentieth-century as the very familiar, "I deserve." I can't be contained here; something else, something better must be provided.

But something is missing in Goethe's bombast. God is absent—or rather, replaced by the author himself. Community has evaporated also. His towering ego shoves fellowship aside, banishes relationships. Nature may assign another form for his existence, but his confinement will be solitary.

In one respect, though, Goethe is on to something.

Surely activity *does* continue beyond the grave. We are "assigned another form of existence."

> *So will it be with the resurrection of the dead. The body that is sown is perishable, it is raised imperishable; it is sown in dishonor, it is raised in glory; it is sown in weakness, it is raised in power; it is sown a natural body, it is raised a spiritual body.*
>
> *1 Corinthians 15:42-44*

This new form is designed for activity. Not serving the demands of the ego, however, but celebrating the virtues of the Creator; not writing in isolated splendor, but embracing the host of fellow celebrants; not demanding of nature the rewards of a lifetime of endeavor, but receiving with gratitude the free awards of grace. What began in life as joyful service to God continues beyond the grave as even more joyful service to God.

That's Heaven. More of the same. Only infinitely better.

More rest

Revelation's picture of an eternal wedding feast tantalizes this preacher. In my ministry, nothing has given me more pleasure than standing before two of our church's young people and pronouncing them husband and wife. Sometimes, admittedly, I conduct weddings that leave me holding my breath, hoping against hope that my fears for this union's success are unfounded. But those apprehensions can't compare with the sheer delight that usually attends these weddings.

But at the end of a hard day, I confess, my favorite description of Heaven is the simplest: Rest.

> *Therefore, since the promise of entering his rest still stands, let us be careful that none of you be found to have fallen short of it.*
>
> *Hebrews 4:1*

> *There remains, then, a Sabbath-rest for the people of God; for anyone who enters God's rest also rests from his own work, just*

as God did from his. Let us, therefore, make every effort to enter
that rest, so that no one will fall by following their example of
disobedience.   *Hebrews 4:9-11*

Hebrews repeatedly exhorts believers to be faithful, to
persevere to the end in spite of current persecution,
because the goal is worth it. As Jesus endured for the joy
set before him (12:1-3), so should we. A reward is waiting
for us. There will be feasting and fellowship and praising—and rest.

In the days of my beginnings as a preacher and teacher,
when existentialism was the rage on campuses, and God's
death was loudly trumpeted in the popular press, I
searched the writings of authors like Albert Camus and
Jean Paul Sartre to find the source of their popularity and,
if it could be found on their pages, truth. For the most
part, it was depressing work. Having declared God dead,
these and other existentialists had to redefine themselves
and all humanity. Denying that man was made in the
image of God, they could only insist that man was made
in no one's image. Each individual had to determine what
it meant to be a human being. As I said, not the best way
to lighten your day.

So great was existentialism's popularity in the 1960s,
though, I was hardly prepared for its reputation three
decades later. By the 1990s, God was thriving and existentialism was dead. Sartre, hero to a generation of aspiring
young intellectuals, was a virtual unknown. I shouldn't
have been surprised. Before he died, even Sartre had
rejected Sartreism. In his autobiography, *Les Mots (The
Words)*, he writes of his precocious childhood and youth
when, turned off by bourgeois Christianity, he sought
refuge in literature and philosophy, in effect making a religion of them. It didn't work, however. With exceptional
frankness, Sartre confesses he had also given up this sub-
stitute religion.

I have caught the Holy Ghost in the cellars and flung him out of them. Atheism is a cruel, long-term business. I have gone through it to the end. I see clearly, I am free from illusions, I know my real tasks, and I must surely deserve a civic prize; for about ten years I have been a man who is waking up, cured of a long, bitter-sweet madness, who cannot get away from it, who cannot recall his old ways without laughing and who no longer has any idea what to do with his life. I have become once again the traveler without a ticket that I was at seven: the ticket-collector has entered my compartment and is looking at me, but less sternly than he once did: in fact, all he wants is to go away and let me complete the journey in peace; as long as I give him a valid excuse of some kind, he will be satisfied. Unfortunately I cannot find one and, besides, do not even want to look for one: we shall go on talking together, will at least, as far as Dijon where I know quite well that no one is waiting for me.[3]

To renounce one's childhood faith is one thing; to labor for ten years clinging to a hollow substitute is quite another. Sartre pushes on in his meaningless journey through life, having no reason for the excursion and no one at the end to welcome him. For Sartre, there is no rest.

Our recent trip to Asia reminded us that the world's major religions promise something at the end of the journey—if not rest, at least an end of suffering. In this brief overview, I'm leaning on Professor Hans Kung's summary. According to him,

- The Chinese generally believe in a world above, to which one's spirit ascends.
- A Hindu's supreme goal is final liberation and redemption from this world's suffering and knowledge of or union with the deity, which results in perfect bliss.

- The Buddhist's Nirvana is a final state without desire, hatred, or blindness. In other words, without suffering. *Some schools of Buddhism, but not many, teach that Nirvana is a purely negative state or total annihilation of the individual; for the majority, individuality is preserved.*
- Christians have been influenced by the great Christian leader Augustine, who concludes his work on the theology of history, *The City of God*, with a discussion "of the great Sabbath, the day of the Lord, the eternal eighth day, which will bring eternal rest of the spirit and the body."4

We have been influenced by Augustine, but we have been inspired by Scriptures like this touch of Heaven in Isaiah 11:6-9:

> *The wolf will live with the lamb,*
> *the leopard will lie down with the goat,*
> *the calf and the lion and the yearling together;*
> *and a little child will lead them.*
> *The cow will feed with the bear,*
> *their young will lie down together,*
> *and the lion will eat straw like the ox.*
> *The infant will play near the hole of the cobra,*
> *and the young child put his hand into the*
> *viper's nest.*
> *They will neither harm nor destroy on all my holy*
> *mountain,*
> *for the earth will be full of the knowledge of the Lord as*
> *the waters cover the sea.*

No strife, no war, no danger. Rest.

May I return once more to C. S. Lewis? Writing to Sheldon Vanauken, an Oxford student groping his way toward faith, Lewis asked the young man how it was that he, "as a product of a materialistic universe, was not at home there?" He raised the question in a now-famous analogy: "Do fish complain of the sea for being wet? Or if they did, would that fact itself not strongly suggest that they had not always been, or would not always be, purely aquatic creatures? Then, if we complain of time and take such joy in the seemingly timeless moment, what does that suggest?"

He answers his own questions:

> It suggests that we have not always been or will not always be purely temporal creatures. It suggests that we were created for eternity. Not only are we harried by time, we seem unable, despite a thousand generations, even to get used to it. We are always amazed at it—how fast it goes, how slowly it goes, how much of it is gone. Where, we cry, has the time gone? We aren't adapted to it, not at home in it. If that is so, it may appear as a proof, or at least a powerful suggestion, that eternity exists and is our home.[5]

So we fight time here, immersed in the struggle for existence, but we dream of that day to come when, the battles over, we can at last rest.

"Blessed are the dead who die in the Lord from now on" Revelation 14:13.

¹Other Scriptures in Revelation add to the picture of the blessed ones:
"Blessed and holy are those who have part in the first resurrection.
The second death has no power over them, but they will be priests
of God and of Christ and will reign with him for a thousand years"
(20:6).
"Blessed is he who keeps the words of the prophecy in this book"
(22:7).
"Blessed are those who wash their robes, that they may have the
right to the tree of life and may go through the gates into the city"
(22:14).

²Quoted by Kathe Kollwitz in *Context,* March 15, 1996, p. 4.

³Quoted in Hans Kung, *Eternal Life.* New York: Doubleday and Company, 1948, pp. 40, 41.

⁴Hans Kung, *Credo.* New York, et al: Doubleday, 1992, pp. 180-182.

⁵Sheldon Vanauken: *A Severe Mercy.* London, et al: Hodder and
Stoughton, 1977, p. 203.

13

The Blessings
of Belief

*Then Jesus told him, "Because you have seen me,
you have believed; blessed are those
who have not seen and yet have believed."*
John 20:29

*"Blessed is the man who does
not fall away on account of me."*
Matthew 11:6

In John 20:29, Jesus is speaking for people like you and
me: "Blessed are those who have not seen and yet have
believed." We're the type James has in mind when, after
encouraging a person to ask for wisdom, he adds, "But
when he asks, he must believe and not doubt, because he
who doubts is like a wave of the sea, blown and tossed by

the wind" (James 1:6). Yes, the doubter in us says, "I be-lieve—or at least I want to believe." But the moment we profess belief, doubt intrudes. "Just how much do you believe, anyway? Where's the proof that what you believe is true? And if you are such a great believer, how can you explain your wavering, your inconsistencies, your all-too-frequent failures to practice the faith you preach?"

We're not peculiar, we who have to struggle to believe. In the Scriptures even a prophet like John the Baptist has his moments. From his prison cell he dispatches his disci-ples to check Jesus out. This is the same man who bap-tized Jesus, who called him the "Lamb of God, who takes away the sin of the world!" (John 1:29). When Jesus appeared at the Jordan for his baptism, John was so cer-tain of Jesus' identity he hesitated to presume. He didn't feel worthy. He was only the forerunner of the Christ; he would decrease while Jesus' power and influence would far surpass his. He was certain of Jesus.

But that was then, and now, as he languishes in prison, John hesitates again. This time it is Jesus he's unsure of. "Could I have been wrong? Did I misjudge this man? Have I jumped to a conclusion? He knows I'm here; why hasn't he rescued me? What am I to make of his silence? Have I promoted a fraud?" He is in prison, but his con-finement doesn't shut out the gossip. Jesus is in trouble with the authorities. His critics are multiplying. John has to know: "Are you the one who was to come, or should we expect someone else?"

Jesus doesn't take offense. He never despises honest questions. He sends John's messengers back with a direct reply: Tell John "what you hear and see: The blind receive sight, the lame walk, those who have leprosy are cured, the deaf hear, the dead are raised, and the good news is preached to the poor." In other words, Isaiah's messianic prophecy is being fulfilled. "Look at my ministry, then compare it with Isaiah 61:1, 2, and you will see I am fulfilling the job description of the promised one."

Then these unexpected words, "Blessed is the man who does not fall away on account of me" (Matthew 11:6). John wasn't wrong to doubt, and he certainly did not sin in seeking evidence. Not in the questioning, but in abandoning faith, is the blessing lost.

Sometimes Jesus does sound as if it's wrong to doubt, as in this verse:

> "I tell you the truth, if you have faith and do not doubt, not only can you do what was done to the fig tree, but also you can say to this mountain, 'Go, throw yourself into the sea,' and it will be done."   Matthew 21:21

And this one:

> "I tell you the truth, if anyone says to this mountain, 'Go, throw yourself into the sea' and does not doubt in his heart but believes that what he says will happen, it will be done for him."
>   Mark 11:23

Is he making a sin of doubting, or is he just stating the obvious, that doubt shuts down the power that faith releases? Did Peter sin when, walking on the water, he turned his eyes from Jesus to the waves and began to sink? Wasn't it rather that he wavered, lost his "grip" and thus his power? Jesus immediately reached out his hand and caught him. "You of little faith," he said, "why did you doubt?" (Matthew 14:31). It is a bit of a scolding, all right. But for this momentary lapse Jesus doesn't banish Peter from his company. His point is more basic: When you were trusting me and walking by faith, you were doing something extraordinary. When doubt took over, you sank.

The person with whom many Christians most identify is the distraught father in Mark 9. Begging Jesus to heal his son of epilepsy, he protests, "I do believe." But then, because he is a man of integrity, he adds, "Help me overcome my unbelief!" (v. 24). He has faith in Jesus—mostly. But complete trust is beyond him right now. He's carried his son to others for healing, but again and again he's been disappointed. With all his heart he wants to believe Jesus can heal the boy, with all his will he determines to trust him, but with all his honesty he has to admit his is a tentative faith. It's the best he can do, under the circumstances. He hopes it's enough.

It is. Jesus heals his son.

Thoughtful faith

God doesn't expect us to stop thinking when we become Christians, or to forget the lessons, sometimes bitter, that life has taught us. "Just trust in Jesus" may sound like good advice, but it doesn't go down well with college students whose childhood faith is being battered by hostile professors. They can't shut down their mental faculties and let something called "blind faith" take over. Not only will they be unable to answer their critics, but they won't be able to satisfy themselves. They have gone to college to learn to think. Professors and peers will challenge every tenet of their creed. They must examine their assumptions and question their conclusions as never before. To think is, by definition, to doubt, to test the answers you've previously accepted, to hear new voices with new perspectives. Without entertaining other possibilities, including the refusal to believe, belief is rendered meaningless or at best innocuous. To choose among options is to doubt some while selecting one, hoping it will prove the right choice. As Philip Toynbee pointed out near the end of his spiritual journey, "How very few holy persons have combined deep spiritual passion with openness of mind and heart. We must try to do both."[1]

This father has no personal proof yet of Jesus' ability. He is hoping what others have told him about the Galilean is true. He is betting his son's health on him.

Jesus promises that those who have not seen and yet believe will be blessed. Who would not want the blessing? What could possibly keep anyone from believing in Jesus as Lord?

Lots of things, it turns out. Let's look at a few.

Jesus is not the only option

George Reiger's picture in the *Arizona Republic* was an eye-stopper.[2] Fortunately, it didn't display his entire body, but his naked back, shoulder, and arm show enough of his 303 Disney-related tattoos to prove he's a true believer in Walt's kingdom. If the photo isn't enough, he offers this explanation: "This is my religion. This is my life. Every cent I have goes to Disney."

What a crazy option—but no crazier than some of the more respectable alternatives people choose. Crystals? Tea leaves? Positioning of the planets? Guidance from the stars? Mumbling mantras? Enigmatic sayings of half-naked gurus? Take your pick.

Or perhaps be content with Mammon, the god of choice among most of your contemporaries. Mammon (Money) has been popular for a long time. Jesus himself warned that you can't serve God and Money. A modern variation of this old-time religion is the New Age, in which a cult of celebrity offers itself for those who have already success-fully snared Mammon for their purposes. What could be more chic than claiming art as your god, high culture as your religion? In these "denominations," silence about the biblical God is strictly enforced, but every conceivable sub-stitute is not only tolerated but encouraged. Could all the beautiful people who espouse some form or other of the New Age be wrong? Could their disdain of all things Waspish (white, Anglo-Saxon, and Protestant) be mere snobbery? Against the intellectual pretensions of these *ersatz* religions, how can the simple gospel message have any appeal?

God's champions are
a pretty disappointing lot

In a favorite *Calvin and Hobbs* cartoon strip, Calvin drops a slice of bread into the toaster, waits, then watches the smoke pour out as the toast burns. "When you think how well basic appliances work," he mutters, "it's hard to believe anyone ever gets on an airplane." As a regular airline commuter, I identify with his sentiment. Hardly a flight goes by that I don't discover some part of the plane (a seat back that won't stay upright, a reading light that won't turn on, a dripping water faucet in the rest room, a sprung spring in the seat cushion) that begs for repair. And these are just the surface parts. I've trained myself not to think about the engine!

Sometimes it's not the mechanics I worry about, but the personnel. On a flight aboard a SAAB 340 not long ago, I sat in the third row, where I could easily see the flight attendant. She was a beautiful young woman of Asian descent, charming, eager to please—and uncertain. When she instructed us over the public address system, she read every word, and she didn't read smoothly. Her stuttering did nothing to ease any anxieties a passenger might have had. If I hadn't been a seasoned veteran of these commuter airlines, I'd have looked for the nearest exit. Her inexperience was so apparent I prayed we wouldn't face any emergency. I doubted she could handle it.

Similarly, what Christian—or would-be Christian—hasn't had his or her faith severely tested by inexperienced or unworthy religious leaders? In recent years a steady stream of scandals has rocked the American religious scene. Men and women who have held sway over thousands, or even millions, of followers have been found out, caught in immorality, and have disappeared in disgrace. They preached one thing but practiced something far different. In other instances, sincere but inexperienced teachers have read from a script, but their greenness and undeveloped skills have encouraged skepticism rather than faith.

Our faith should be in Christ and not in his inept disciples. Sometimes, however, those disciples obstruct the path to the Lord. Seekers can't get to him. In doubt they turn away.

Jesus' demands are too tough

Doubting is easier than obeying. The easy-believism so popular in America, whether it's the so-called "civil religion" that's paraded every election season or the New Age cults or any other alternative religion, is popular precisely because it demands so little of the adherents. God is asked to bless us—as a nation, as a church, as a businessman embarking on a new enterprise, as a wife struggling with her difficult husband, as a patient facing an uncertain prognosis—but no one is asked to do anything for God.

When people fully grasp what it means to believe in Jesus, even more, to be his disciple, the deserters scurry to the nearest exit under a cover of proclaimed doubts.

At one point in his ministry, as he watched some of his erstwhile disciples walk away, Jesus gave the twelve permission to desert also. "You do not want to leave too, do you?" Peter assured him they wouldn't, because there wasn't anyone else to turn to. "You have the words of eternal life" (John 6:67, 68).

Jesus would not mislead them, however. Following him would be hard. They'd need help. "This is why I told you that no one can come to me unless the Father has enabled him" (John 6:63-68). Exactly what blessings, then, does Jesus have in mind for those who, not having seen, believe? He doesn't say, at least in so many words. Each chapter in this book has lifted up one or more of them. In this concluding chapter, let me mention a few more. Every one deserves fuller treatment. And, even then, there would

be more to tell. Such is the abundance Jesus promises.
What follows is my personal, rather peculiar, list.

Blessing: You don't fall for just anything

Was it G. K. Chesterton who warned that the problem
with banishing God from your life is not that you now
believe in nothing, but that you may fall for anything? To
reject Christ as Lord of your life does not mean you won't
have a lord; it just means Christ won't be the one. Some
people, you know, are pretty serious about Elvis. As we
saw above, for George Reiger, Disney is lord. The proliferation of cults today is proof positive that even though for
many people God is dead, gods aren't.

Blessing: You are able to see the big picture

Religious persons are often condemned as narrow-
minded bigots. My personal experience with genuine
believers has left me marveling rather at the depth of their
understanding, the breadth of their perspective. They live
in a big world; it encompasses all reality, limited by neither time nor space. Having learned to view the world
through God's eyes, they are no longer trapped by what
Steven Rockefeller calls "those illusions, those rationaliza-
tions, those prejudices, those attachments, which distort
our relationship to the world." He says that "that kind of
other worldliness has a certain constructive function. One
sometimes has to withdraw in order to enter more fully
into the world."[3] The believer can be in the world but not
of it, a participant in his culture but not bound by its bor-
ders. His biblical perspective keeps him from being fooled
by or trapped in thought categories that rule the world
about him.

Blessing: You are on the right side

You may have heard of the deaf man who never missed
a worship service at his church. Every Sunday his less con-

scientious neighbors noted his departure from home,
dressed in his Sunday-go-to-meeting best. When one of
them could contain herself no longer, she asked him (probably by writing the question on his pad). "Why do you go
to church? You can't hear a word of the sermon and you
can't even hear the music. What do you get out of it? Why
bother?"

"Because," he patiently explained, "I want people to
know which side I'm on."

Stephen Carter's position is the same:

> A religion . . . is not simply a means for under-
> standing one's self, or even of contemplating the
> nature of the universe, or existence, or of anything
> else. A religion is, at its heart, a way of denying the
> authority of the rest of the world; it is a way of saying
> to fellow human beings and to the state those fellow
> humans have erected, "No, I will not accede to your
> will."[4]

Jesus' disciples are charged with the same assignment:
Let the world know whose side you are on. Resist the
pressures to make you conform to its will. Though in the
world, you are not under its control. You obey a higher
authority. Enjoy your freedom—and at the same time
shine a light showing others how to find it. Of course, you
must not be foolish enough to expect the world to appreci-
ate your liberty. You don't expect better treatment than
your Lord received, do you? "If the world hates you, keep
in mind that it hated me first" (John 15:18).

Jesus asked his Father to protect his disciples. He knew
we'd all be in for trouble, because "they are not of the
world, even as I am not of it" (John 17:16). Not to worry,
though, because "everyone born of God overcomes the
world. This is the victory that has overcome the world,
even our faith" (1 John 5:4).

The best of blessings: Blessed assurance

I'll date myself with this one. Today's chorus-singing
youngsters don't recognize the name of Fanny Crosby, let
alone sing any of her hundreds of songs, many of which
were staples in the churches my generation grew up in.
For us, one is irreplaceable:

> Blessed assurance, Jesus is mine!
> Oh, what a foretaste of glory divine!
> Heir of salvation, purchase of God,
> Born of His Spirit, washed in His blood.
>
> This is my story, this is my song,
> Praising my Savior all the day long;
> This is my story, this is my song,
> Praising my Savior all the day long.

Admittedly, Garrison Keillor is no Fanny Crosby, but in
his *We Are Still Married* he recommends a little faith to see
you through. He asks, what else except faith will do in
such "a cynical, corrupt time? When the country goes temporarily to the dogs, cats must learn to be circumspect,
walk on fences, sleep in trees, and have faith that all this
woofing is not the last word."[5]

Our blessed assurance is that the last word is "a living
hope through the resurrection of Jesus Christ from the
dead, and into an inheritance that can never perish, spoil
or fade—kept in heaven" for us (1 Peter 1:3, 4)

We can face whatever we must face with confidence.

When his doctor confirmed that Ron Mehl, a Beaverton,
Oregon, pastor, had leukemia, he was flabbergasted. He
knew about leukemia. As a minister he had prayed for
many cancer patients. But like the rest of us, he couldn't
believe it had happen to him. He said it was as if someone
had flipped through the pages of his life's book, turned to
the last chapter, and handed it to him to read. He didn't
want to know the ending, certainly not so soon. He asked

all the questions you or I would ask: Where do I turn? Who do I tell? What should I say? What shouldn't I say?

Before long, the word was out. Then he had to face those well-meaning but irritating people who confidently claim they have a clear word from the Lord for the patient:

"It's just a test of your faith. A pathway to growth."

"Your problem is a lack of faith."

"There is sin in your life."

"You shouldn't be a pastor."

"You're out of the will of God."

"How can you minister to someone who's sick when you need healing yourself?"

The best word he received, though, came in a quiet moment with his wife, Joyce. Taking him in her arms, she held him close. "How are you doing and what do you think?" he asked her, as concerned about her well-being as his own.

She answered with only a sentence, but it was enough: "The servant of the Lord is indestructible until God is through with him."[6]

"Blessed are those who have not seen and yet have believed."

---

[1]*End of a Journey.* London: Bloomsbury Publishing Company, 1988, p. 267.

[2]Friday, October 28, 1994, p. A7.

[3]Bill Moyers, *A World of Ideas.* New York, et al: Doubleday, 1990, p. 174.

[4]Stephen L. Carter, *The Culture of Disbelief.* New York: Basic Books, a div. of Harper Collins, 1993, p. 41.

[5]Quoted in *Context,* April 1, 1993, p. 6.

[6]Ron Mehl, *Surprise Endings.* Sisters, Oregon: Multnomah Books, Questar Publishers; copyright 1993 by Ron Mehl, pp. 16, 17.